Math Intervention

Building Number Power

with Formative Assessments, Differentiation, and Games

Grades 3-5

Jennifer Taylor-Cox, Ph.D.

EYE ON EDUCATION
6 DEPOT WAY WEST, SUITE 106
LARCHMONT, NY 10538
(914) 833-0551
(914) 833-0761 fax
www.eyeoneducation.com

Library of Congress Cataloging-in-Publication Data

Taylor-Cox, Jennifer.
Math intervention : building number power with formative
assessments, differentiation, and games, Grades 3-5 / Jennifer Taylor-Cox.
      p. cm.
ISBN 978-1-59667-112-6
1. Mathematics--Study and teaching (Elementary) 2. Mathematical readiness.
3. Group guidance in education. I. Title.
QA135.6.T3565 2008
372.7--dc22

                                        2008046896

10   9   8   7   6   5   4   3

Book design services provided by
Jennifer Osterhouse Graphic Design
3752 Danube Drive, Davidsonville, MD 21035
(410-798-8585)

Also available from Eye On Education

Math Intervention:
Building Number Power with Formative Assessments,
Differentiation, and Games, Grades PreK-2
Jennifer Taylor-Cox

Family Math Night: Math Standards in Action
Jennifer Taylor-Cox

Family Math Night: Middle School Math Standards in Action
Jennifer Taylor-Cox and Christine Oberdorf

Mathematics Coaching Handbook:
Working with Teachers to Improve Instruction
Pia M. Hansen

Differentiated Instruction for K-8 Math and Science:
Activities and Lesson Plans
Mary Hamm and Dennis Adams

A Collection of Performance Tasks and Rubrics:
Primary School Mathematics
Charlotte Danielson and Pia Hansen Powell

Upper Elementary School Mathematics
Charlotte Danielson

Middle School Mathematics
Charlotte Danielson

High School Mathematics
Charlotte Danielson and Elizabeth Marquez

Mathematics and Multi-Ethnic Students: Exemplary Practices
Yvelyne Germain-McCarthy & Katharine Owens

Assessment in Middle and High School Mathematics:
A Teacher's Guide
Daniel Brahier

Teaching Mathematics in the Block
Susan Gilkey and Carla Hunt

Acknowledgements

This book is dedicated to Joey Cox.
Thanks for all of the hours spent playing math games with me.
I enjoyed every minute.

● ● ● ● ● ● ● ● ● ● ● ● ● ●

Appreciation is extended to friend and colleague, Christine Oberdorf,
an exemplary mathematics educator and incredible staff development teacher.
Thank you for your brain power and your friendship.

Gratitude is expressed to friend and colleague, Karren Schultz-Ferrell, an expert
in early childhood mathematics. Thank you for your generous feedback.

Recognition is extended to friend and colleague, Sheila Etzkorn, an amazing
math educator. You are an inspiration to students and teachers.

Special thanks to friend and colleague, Shirley Sneed, an excellent staff
development teacher. Thanks for your knowledge and support.

Thanks to other reviewers Alice Gabbard, Brenda Love,
Gary Martin, and Virginia Newlin.

Tons of appreciation is offered to Jennifer Osterhouse, a brilliant graphic designer.
It is my honor and pleasure to work with you.

Gratitude is expressed to Marida Hines, a talented illustrator.
Thank you for your artistic perspective.

Extensive acknowledgment and gratitude are offered to the thousands of
students, educators, and parents who have influenced my life. It is for
you and because of you that this essential work is done.

Believe in the power of math!
Jennifer Taylor-Cox

About the Author

 Dr. Jennifer Taylor-Cox is an enthusiastic, captivating presenter and well-known educator. She is the Executive Director of **Taylor-Cox Instruction, LLC**. Jennifer serves as a consultant in mathematics education providing professional development opportunities for numerous districts across the United States. Her keynote speeches, workshops, seminars, classroom demonstration lessons, and presentations are always high-energy and insightful.

Jennifer earned her Ph.D. from the University of Maryland and was awarded the "Outstanding Doctoral Research Award" from the University of Maryland and the "Excellence in Teacher Education Award" from Towson University. She served as the president of the Maryland Council of Teachers of Mathematics. Jennifer is the author of many professional articles and books including *Family Math Night: Math Standards in Action* and *Family Math Night: Middle School Math Standards in Action*.

Dr. Taylor-Cox knows how to make learning mathematics engaging and fun which motivates learners of all ages! She has a passion for differentiated math instruction. Jennifer believes that all students are entitled to targeted instruction aimed at their specific learning needs. Jennifer lives and has her office in Severna Park, Maryland. She is the mother of three children. Jennifer truly understands how to connect research and practice in education. Her zeal for mathematics education is alive in her work with educators, students, and parents.

If you are interested in learning more about the professional development opportunities Dr. Taylor-Cox offers, please feel free to contact her at **Taylor-Cox Instruction, LLC**.

Jennifer Taylor-Cox, Ph.D., Educational Consultant
Office: 410-729-5599, Fax: 410-729-3211
Email: Jennifer@Taylor-CoxInstruction.com

Free Downloads

The 35 games displayed in this book are also available on Eye On Education's Web site as Adobe Acrobat PDF files. Those who have purchased this book have permission to download them and print them out. You can access these downloads by visiting Eye On Education's Web site: **www.eyeoneducation.com**.

Click on **FREE Downloads** or search or browse our Web site to find this book and then scroll down for downloading instructions.

You'll need your book-buyer access code: MAI-7112-6

Table of Contents

Introduction

What is Math Intervention?

Math intervention is targeted instruction for students struggling with mathematics. Too often students have difficulty understanding math concepts, and the instruction they receive perpetuates or masks the problems rather than addressing them. Students are left to flail and founder in a confusing sea of procedures and rules. The problems become more profound as the student moves into each new grade. As math educators we can no longer let this happen. We must make math meaningful for students and provide targeted instruction that focuses on the precise academic needs of students. It is essential that we concentrate on repairing students' misconceptions and learning gaps in ways that build their math capacity.

In mathematics there are four interconnected goals; accuracy, efficiency, flexibility, and fluency. Our first priority is to help students with their math accuracy, which means we help them learn how to obtain the correct answer. Next, we address efficiency by helping students learn how to obtain the right answer as quickly as possible as is appropriate for the concept. After correctness and speed, we help students improve flexibility so that they understand how to apply their learning to new situations and in different ways. Flexibility means adaptability. We want students to be able to revise and adjust their thinking in ways that maintain and increase accuracy and efficiency. Finally, we must support students as they build their fluency with mathematics. Fluency relates to the confidence and ease with which students work with mathematics concepts.

Accuracy, efficiency, flexibility, and fluency are goals built upon one another within each math concept. Accuracy comes first because there is no point in having any of the other goals without exactness. We do not want students to increase speed if they are getting the answers wrong. Likewise, there is little need to be flexible and fluent with incorrect answers. Educators should focus on accuracy first, even when it takes a long time for students to come up with the correct answer. As soon as students have established accuracy, we need to move right on to focus on efficiency. Our goal is to help students learn how to maintain accuracy while increasing speed. As soon as the students quickly obtain the right answers, we want to focus on flexibility by providing new situations that require changes in their thinking. The fluency aspect of mathematics can be addressed during any of the three previous goals. We can build students' fluency while increasing accuracy, efficiency, and flexibility.

Think about this scenario. A student is trying to solve the following division problem; Sixty-seven boxes of cookies. The boxes of cookies are packed in cartons. Each carton holds 8 boxes of cookies. How many cartons are needed to pack all the boxes of cookies? The student tackles this problem using a *guess and check* strategy. She starts with 100 cartons and figures out ten cartons hold 800 cookies. Because 800 are way too many, she tries 50 cartons. Then she tries ten cartons followed by nine cartons. She tries eight cartons and realizes there are some leftover boxes of cookies, so she tries nine cartons again. The strategy worked because her answer is correct; therefore, she has accuracy. Yet, the *guess and check* strategy was quite time consuming. If we teach this student to use *repeated subtraction*, her speed will increase. Beginning with 67, she subtracts eight, then eight more, then eight more, and so on until she has three boxes left. She knows these boxes also need a carton and comes up with the correct answer to the problem. She has maintained accuracy and increased her speed.

To help this student move to flexibility, we can encourage her to consider *fact families* and *inverse operations*. She knows 8 x 8 = 64 and therefore can apply this knowledge to the division situation. Furthering her flexibility, she compares 64 to 67 and accurately and efficiently finds that nine cartons are needed to hold 67 boxes of cookies. Her confidence and ease have increased based upon the successful experiences.

Timing is very important. Sometimes well-meaning math educators jump too fast to efficiency and flexibility. They impose all of these rules and procedures with intentions of helping students see efficient and flexible ways to solve problems. However, teaching rules and procedures is not the same as teaching concepts. Understanding what to do is not enough. We must teach students why a procedure works so that they better understand the concept. If we only teach rules and procedures, struggling students typically achieve random accuracy (if they remember the rules and procedures) and rarely achieve flexibility or fluency because they do not truly own the knowledge. Math educators need to teach concepts to help students build foundations so that they can understand the math. When concepts are ignored and the focus is solely on rules and procedures, struggling students often develop misconceptions and learning gaps. However, if students understand concepts, it is appropriate to help them increase speed and flexibility by teaching rules and procedures, but we must include reasons and connections to help students make this math meaningful.

Students may return to inefficient strategies when faced with challenging problems. They do so because they want to achieve accuracy. These students benefit from the teacher providing intervention that targets their exact academic needs while challenging them to increase accuracy, efficiency, flexibility, and fluency. While it makes sense to focus first on accuracy then move to efficiency, flexibility, and fluency, the goals are not isolated. We often move back and forth, teaching all four goals at the same time to help students understand the hows and whys of mathematics.

Focus on Number Sense and Computation

Typically, the problems that struggling students have in mathematics relate to number sense and computation. Number sense involves an expansive and inclusive understanding of number and operations that allows a person to make sound judgments and utilize practical and effective math strategies (McIntosh, Reys, & Reys 1993). Number sense is not something that a person has or does not have. Number sense can be taught through a concept-based approach. It is important to examine all of the aspects of number sense to identify which of these concepts our struggling students are missing. General intervention is not the best way to build students' number sense. We must build students' number sense through targeted intervention aimed at the students' exact academic needs.

The *Focal Points* in mathematics for the elementary grades highlight number and operations as critically important and consistent areas of concentration (NCTM 2006). All of the concepts in this book are interrelated components of number sense and operations. This focus on specific concepts does not imply that we need to teach math concepts in isolation. Productive mathematics instruction is inclusive, interconnected, and rich. A focus on number sense and computation concepts in math intervention helps us identify and address gaps and misconceptions that students have in their understanding of mathematics. Intervention does not replace math instruction. Intervention is in addition to good mathematics instruction.

What Makes Math Intervention Successful?

Students who struggle in mathematics need explicit instruction. Explicit instruction is provided when teachers give students ongoing feedback, clear models, a variety of examples, time for practice, and opportunities to talk through the hows and whys of the math situation (National Mathematics Advisory Panel 2008). Successful math intervention is precise and focused on students' immediate learning needs.

Diagnosing and addressing students' needs are part of Response-to-Intervention (RTI). Although the use of RTI is common practice in language arts, RTI is completely applicable to mathematics, as well. RTI promotes the identification and diagnosis of potential learning problems by analyzing students' responses to instruction and providing corrective feedback. With RTI students are offered specific interventions and progress is frequently monitored. Tier 2 (small group) and Tier 3 (individual) are excellent group structures for providing the specific interventions presented in this book. Successful mathematics intervention applies the structure of RTI—identify, diagnose, and address students' learning weaknesses early and precisely.

There are several other key components that make math intervention successful. The group structure, quantity and quality of the tasks, use of new strategies, educator's expertise, incorporation of problem solving, and student's level of motivation are some of the factors that influence math intervention success.

Productive math intervention is rarely a whole class endeavor. Math intervention is most effective in small group structures. Students are more likely to reveal gaps in understanding and misconceptions when they are in small groups. Teachers are more likely to find these gaps and misunderstandings when they are working with a small group. Furthermore, the small group structure allows teachers to target the instruction more effectively because they can constantly adjust the instruction. Teachers can tailor the interaction and math discourse to help struggling students find success. Small group instruction provides opportunities for strategic mathematics intervention.

When possible, one-on-one instruction has powerful potential. The teacher can concentrate completely on one student's academic needs. For some of us, one-on-one instruction is only possible in small chunks of time because we have an entire class to teach. For others such as special educators, tutors, paraeducators, assistants, parents, and volunteers, one-on-one instruction is more common. The benefits of one-on-one instruction can be great because this structure provides opportunities for intensive intervention. Students are typically highly engaged and they gain confidence in their abilities.

More is better is not necessarily true when it comes to math intervention. It really depends on what you mean by *more*. A packet of 100 math problems does not make a better mathematics student. More problems do not necessarily help students, especially if students are left alone to solve page after page of problems. In these cases, all the students typically learn is that they are not good at solving math problems—worse yet, that they hate math. To make the *more is better* idea beneficial for struggling students, consider more time, more instruction, more strategies, and more opportunities for success. These are the ingredients needed for successful math intervention.

Drill does kill. It kills the spirit of learning (Taylor-Cox & Kelly 2008). Too much drill is boring, isolated, and unproductive. Struggling students do not need stacks of flash cards. They need motivating math games that provide them with multiple opportunities for learning. Struggling students must have experiences that help them understand the math, not empty, meaningless experiences. They need context and connections so they learn to own the mathematics.

Certainly, struggling students do not need more of the same. Obviously, the original instruction did not work; otherwise they would not be struggling. Struggling students need new strategies and experiences beyond the textbook. We must offer our struggling students targeted instruction aimed at fortifying specific math concepts for students. Struggling students benefit from new and creative ways in which to learn the information.

An educator's expertise plays an important role in successful math intervention for struggling students. One of the recommendations made on the recent report given by the National Mathematics Advisory Panel involves the expertise of mathematics educators. The panel recommends that "teachers must know in detail the mathematical content they are responsible for teaching and its connections to other important mathematics topics, both prior to and beyond the level they are assigned to teach (2008 p. 37). Educators must understand the concepts, know which concepts the student needs to work on, and know how to assess the level of understanding the student currently has. Good educators strive to increase their levels of expertise. They gain knowledge through their classroom experiences, pedagogical discourse with other educators, and using a variety of resources. Those providing math intervention can be a veteran or new classroom teacher, special educator, ELL teacher, paraeducator, instructional assistant, teacher aide, volunteer, tutor, and/or parent. The point is for educators to have the expertise and resources necessary to provide successful math intervention for students.

Successful math intervention includes problem solving that is interwoven, not a separate component. The goals are to enable students to build understanding, apply and adapt high-quality strategies, and to evaluate and reflect as they solve math problems (NCTM 2000). When students are engaged in meaningful mathematics, they become better problem solvers. Problem solving is embedded within a math situation when students use various strategies, make decisions, and evaluate their thinking.

The level of motivation and commitment that a student has influences the effectiveness of math intervention. Games motivate and empower students. Games open up multiple opportunities for meaningful mathematics, and they are fun. If given a choice, most students would choose to play a game rather than solve math problems on a page in a textbook. Yet the game may actually teach them more about math than they even realize. That's the beauty of games! They are so entertaining that the learning doesn't seem like a chore. This is not to imply that the math will always be easy. Challenges and increased difficulty are important parts of learning mathematics. Math games can be challenging and enjoyable because games serve as a productive way to hook students into successfully engaging in mathematics. The games in this book provide opportunities for students to learn new concepts, practice skills, and apply math thinking to new situations.

How to Use Formative Assessment

Using formative assessment allows us to know what to teach. Formative assessment provides information about what a student currently knows. We can use the formative assessment data to focus on the explicit academic needs of the students.

"Teachers' regular use of formative assessment improves their students' learning, especially if teachers have additional guidance on using the assessment to design and individualize instruction" (National Mathematics Advisory Panel 2008 p. xxiii). Formative assessment comes in a variety of forms. Sometimes it is a performance task. Other times it is a problem or question. Using a formative assessment that is not too time-consuming allows us to devote as much time as possible to the instruction. Interestingly, using formative assessments can actually save time because the information helps the teacher target the instruction. Each of the concepts presented in this book include a formative assessment that will allow the teacher to uncover and focus on the academic needs of the students.

Monitor Progress

Monitoring students' progress is critically important. As educators we must constantly analyze the progress of students. To accomplish this we need to ask questions:

- Is the student making progress?
- What does the student need to learn next?
- How solid is the student's understanding?
- Does the student need more work with a specific concept?
- Is the student having difficulty maintaining and utilizing specific concepts?
- What misconceptions does the student have?
- Where are the learning gaps?
- Is the student's knowledge incomplete? If so, what is missing?

The answers to these questions help us monitor the progress of students. As we monitor progress, we make decisions about how to target the instruction to meet the exact academic needs of the students.

Struggling students need to understand their progress. As educators monitor the progress of students, they should share it with the students. One way to do so is to regularly meet with students and share evidence of the students' gains in knowledge. The evidence may be formative assessment data and/or the actual preassessments and postassessments. The evidence may be a copy of the game board with notes about what a student did to solve problems or a paper that shows how a student used specific concepts and strategies. Many educators use these and other types of evidence to evaluate a student's performance. The key is to provide constant feedback by sharing this information with the student.

Additional ways to help students monitor their own progress include recording the things they know about the concept, have done with the concept, and goals they have related to the concept *(see page 14 for monitoring tool)*. It is also important for students to evaluate the degree of knowledge of any given concept. Using personal scales to report levels of knowledge is beneficial. To do so, the student places X on a scale (the scale on the monitoring tool is 0-10, but any scale is fine) and dates the X underneath. Later, the student adds other Xs and dates to the scale to show progress. Scales offer a productive way to help students focus on their progress.

A former student, Tony, started the school year struggling in mathematics. He had many misconceptions and learning gaps. We worked on building his understanding of specific math concepts by implementing targeted instruction and playing math games to build conceptual knowledge. Evidence of Tony's progress was archived in an accordion folder. The preassessments were stapled to the post-assessments to highlight progress. One day Tony was proudly going through the folder. I took the opportunity to join him and we celebrated his progress. After looking through the papers, Tony announced, "I really learned a lot. I can't believe it all fits in my brain!"

Positive ways to share progress with students also include highlighting what they have learned and noting what they need to work on next. The educator may say to the student, "You really improved your accuracy and speed with doubles. The next concept we will focus on is near doubles." The idea is to celebrate what the student has learned and set the next goals.

Reteach

Sometimes students do not learn what they need to learn during regular classroom instruction or intervention. In these cases, we must focus on reteaching. Effective reteaching is not teaching the exact same thing in the exact same way again and again. If students are not learning, we identify the concept and present it in a different way. It may be necessary to move back to a previous concept to build foundations. Or, we may need to reveal and address a misconception. Reteaching should be targeted to meet the explicit academic needs of the students. If a student does not understand fact families, telling the student, in a louder voice, what fact families are is not effective reteaching! Instead, we must try new ways to help the student visualize and model fact families. It may also be that the student needs more work with addition and subtraction concepts. The point is to make the reteaching match the immediate needs of the student.

How to Use This Book

We need to know and understand each concept so that we can identify and focus on specific instruction. This book is designed to give math educators the tools to provide direct math intervention in the areas of number sense and computation.

Students who struggle in mathematics deserve personalized math intervention. Knowing which number concepts a student is lacking (whether the student is eight years old or twelve years old) is critical. It is not one-size-fits-all math intervention. A fifth grader may be struggling with third grade concepts. The point is not to focus so much on the grade level; instead we should focus on the specific concepts that the student needs to learn.

Each math concept presented in this book includes a brief description to provide the educator with background information aimed at increasing expertise. In essence, all of these concepts are connected. Therefore, many of the games include multiple concepts. However, each concept is highlighted independently to enable the educator to target instruction for students.

A formative assessment is provided for each concept to help the educator find out if the student has gaps in understanding the concept or if the student has a solid understanding of the concept. Sometimes exact quantities and specific numbers are provided. Other times choices are provided. The intent is for the formative assessments to serve as tools for targeted instruction.

Successful strategies are included with each number concept for the purpose of offering helpful hints and directions. A math word box accompanies each concept to provide potential math words that should be modeled by the educator and used by the students. These are not vocabulary words to be taught in isolation. Instead, these are conceptually rich math words that should be used in context.

To further promote math discourse and math thinking, sample questions are included. Each question represents a different *level of cognitive demand.* Using Bloom's (1956) taxonomy for structure, a sample question is listed for recall, comprehension, application, analysis, evaluation, and synthesis. The simplest question (recall) is listed first, followed by increasingly advanced levels of questions through the highest level of cognitive demand needed (synthesis). *Note: While Bloom's (1956) original work suggested evaluation as the highest level, my experience with using the levels of cognitive demand suggests synthesizing is more difficult than evaluating. In addition, some questions could represent more than one level of cognitive demand.* The educator should decide which level of questioning best suits the student's needs at the time. Students should be encouraged to ask questions, too.

To motivate students and activate learning, a math game that directly connects to the specific concept is offered. During the game, the educator should encourage students to use math words, ask questions, and explain and justify their thinking. Each game lists necessary materials and step-by-step directions. Each game is intended to be a springboard for active learning. The educator may modify instruction based on how the student responds to various components of the game.

Each game includes potential content differentiation. If the student has too much difficulty with the concept, the educator is invited to differentiate the content of the game for the student by *moving back* to an easier version of the game. If the student understands the concept, the educator is invited to differentiate the content of the game for the student by *moving ahead* to a more complex version.

This math intervention book is a tool for educators. The book includes addition and subtraction through multifaceted number concepts designed for third through fifth grade students. The companion book *Math Intervention: Building Number Power with Formative Assessments, Differentiation, and Games (Grades PreK-2)* includes early number concepts through addition and subtraction concepts. It is necessary to include addition and subtraction concepts in both books because these ideas are critical to both grade level bands. There may even be situations where both books are needed. Some students may need to begin with the early number concepts. Other students may start with addition and subtraction concepts. The point is to use the formative assessments to find out exactly what the students need...and let the games begin!

_____'s Math Progress

Date/s: _____

Concept: _____

Things I know about this concept:

_____

_____

Things I have done with this concept:

_____

_____

Goals:

_____

_____

_____

How much I know about this concept;
(place X on the scale with date underneath to show level of knowledge; 10 = complete knowledge)

●_____●

0   10

CHAPTER

Addition and Subtraction Concepts

Total and Parts
Counting On and Counting Back
Joining Sets
Number Line Proficiency
Take Away Subtraction
Missing Part Subtraction
Comparison Subtraction
Adding and Subtracting Tens
Adding Doubles and Near Doubles
Fact Families—Addition and Subtraction
Partial Sums
Partial Differences
Near Tens for Addition and Subtraction
Equal Differences

Total and Parts

What is the Total and Parts Concept?

The total and parts concept encourages students to see the parts of whole numbers. By focusing on total and parts, students learn about addition and subtraction. They begin to understand that the parts make the total and that the total is made of parts. The beauty of teaching total and parts is that we can present early addition and subtract concepts at the same time rather than teaching these operations separately.

Formative Assessment

To find out if a student understands total and parts, ask the student to describe the total and parts of the following trains of cubes;

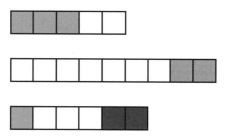

Notice if the student provides the total and parts in the descriptions. If the student is successful, try different parts and larger totals. Identify which totals and parts the students know and which they do not know.

Successful Strategies

Interchange addition and subtraction ideas as students work with total and parts. Encourage students to read aloud and record the parts and total. Using different colors to show the parts often helps students better identify the parts. Grouping the parts is also beneficial. As students gain comfort with total and parts begin working with more than two parts of each total.

> ### Math Words to Use
>
> **total, whole, parts,
> addition, subtraction**

Questions at Different *Levels of Cognitive Demand*

EASY

Recall: *What is the total?*

Comprehension: *How do the parts relate to the total?*

Application: *How could you show different parts of the total?*

Analysis: *How could you compare the parts of more than one total?*

Evaluation: *What helps you understand the parts of a total?*

COMPLEX   **Synthesis:** *What if the total had many parts?*

Big Top Twelve

A game designed to build the concept of total and parts

Materials:

- Die (labeled 1-6 with numerals)
- Crayons or colored pencils
- Big Top Twelve Game Board for each player

Directions:

1. The first player rolls the die. The number showing is one part of twelve.

2. The player decides which Big Top she wants to use to show the part. The player colors the part with a specific color. For example, if the player rolls five, she colors five rectangles (next to one another) in one of the Big Tops with a black crayon.

3. The next player rolls and colors the part of twelve on her game board.

4. Players take turns rolling and coloring parts of twelve. Each new part of the Big Top is shown using a different color.

5. The number rolled cannot be split. If the number rolled cannot be played, the player loses her turn.

6. The first person to complete all three Big Tops is the winner.

Content Differentiation:

Moving Back: Try Big Tops that are less than 12.

Moving Ahead: Play Big Top Twelve without the game board. Each time a number is rolled, it becomes part of one of three addition equations. For example, $2 + 3 + 5 + 2 = 12$. Try other Big Top values.

Big Top Twelve Game Board

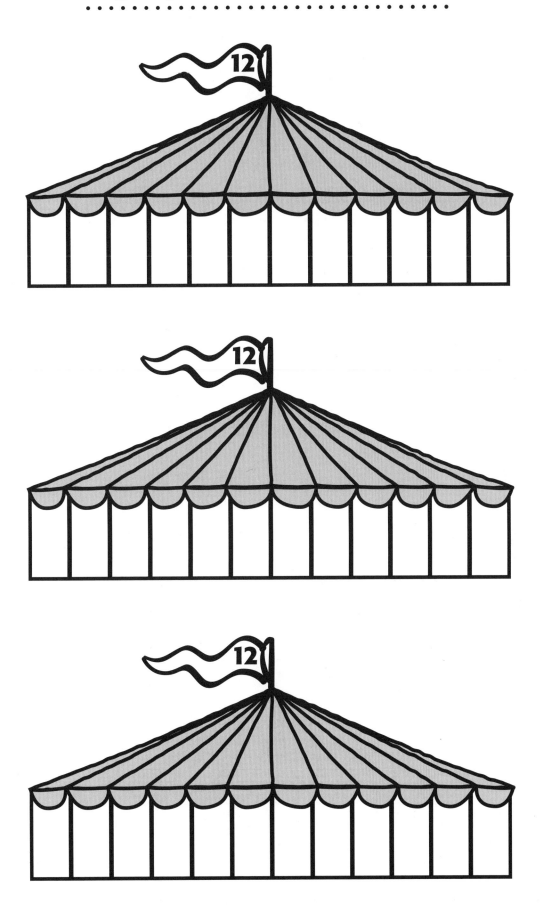

Big Top Twelve Game Board

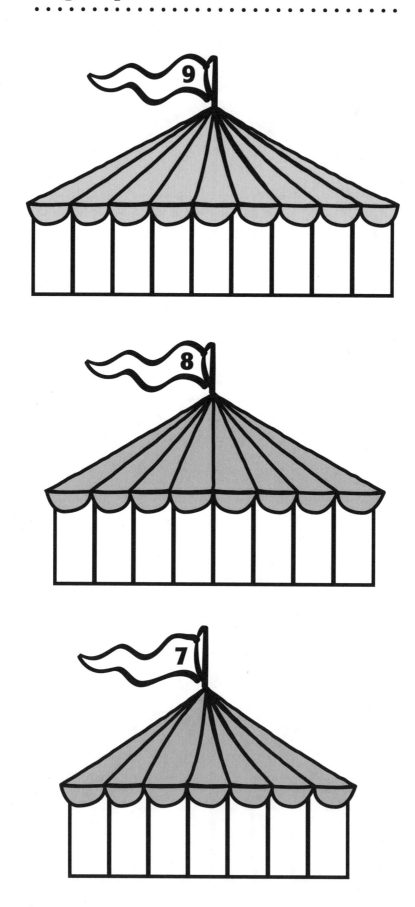

Big Top Twelve Game Board

Counting On and Counting Back

What are Counting On and Counting Back?

Counting on and counting back are strategies that help students with addition and subtraction. Counting on and counting back are efficient strategies when the addition equation is +1, +2, or +3 and when the subtraction equation is -1, -2, or -3. In a situation such as 48 + 23, counting on by ones is not the most efficient strategy because it is too time consuming. Students need to know how to count on and count back, but they also need to judge when it is a good idea to count on or count back.

Formative Assessment

To find out if a student can count on and count back ask the student to name one more than several given numbers (23, 57, 79). Then try two more, three more, one less, two less, and three less.

23 and one more	57 and one more	79 and one more
23 and two more	57 and two more	79 and two more
23 and three more	57 and three more	79 and three more
One less than 23	One less than 57	One less than 79
Two less than 23	Two less than 57	Two less than 79
Three less than 23	Three less than 57	Three less than 79

Identify which situations the students answer correctly and how quickly the students respond to determine how comfortable the students are with counting on and counting back by ones.

Successful Strategies

Identifying when it is efficient and when it is not efficient to use counting on and counting back is just as important as knowing how to count on and count back. When students know how and when to count on by ones, we can introduce counting on by numbers other than one. As discussed previously, counting on by ones is not an efficient strategy to use to solve $48 + 23$; although it would be efficient to count on by tens and then ones to solve the equation ($48 + 23 = 48 + 10 + 10 + 1 + 1 + 1$). Similarly, students can count on by other numbers when they are ready.

> ## Math Words to Use
>
> **count on, count back,
> one more, two more,
> three more, one less,
> two less, three less**

Questions at Different *Levels of Cognitive Demand*

EASY

Recall: *What is one more?*

Comprehension: *What does counting back mean?*

Application: *When is it a good idea to count on by ones?*

Analysis: *How are counting on and counting back similar?*

Evaluation: *When and why is counting back a good strategy?*

Synthesis: *How could you use skip counting by fives to count on?*

COMPLEX

Nifty Fifty

A game designed to build the concepts of counting on and counting back

Materials:

PLAYERS: 2 OR MORE

- Die (labeled 1, 1, 2, 2, 3, 3)
- Nifty Fifty Score Sheet for each player

Directions:

1. All players record 50 in the "start" column of the first round on their score sheets.
2. The first player rolls the die and records the rolled number on his score sheet. The player chooses whether to count on or count back the number rolled and records the "end" number.
3. The next player rolls, records on her score sheet, and counts on or counts back to find the "end" number.
4. The "end" number becomes the start number for each new round.
5. The player who has 50 after the 10th round is the winner.
6. If no players have 50 after the 10th round, the player who is closest to 50 is the winner.

Content Differentiation:

Moving Back: **Change the start/goal number to 20. Write the equation for each round.**

Moving Ahead: **Play Nifty Fifty without the score sheet. Mentally keep track of "start" and "end" numbers. Try greater start/goal numbers or add more rounds.**

Nifty Fifty Score Sheet

Round	Start	Rolled	End
1st			
2nd			
3rd			
4th			
5th			
6th			
7th			
8th			
9th			
10th			

What is the Joining Sets Concept?

Joining sets is an addition concept. Joining sets involves combining quantities and finding the total. Each set that we join is considered an addend. The total of the combined sets is the sum. For some students, the introduction of symbols (+, =), equation formats, and rules come before they have established an understanding of what it means to join sets. These students often struggle with addition because they are trying to remember symbols, formats, and rules that are meaningless to them. It is critical that we help students develop a true understanding of joining sets so that the symbols, formats, and rules make sense to them.

Formative Assessment

To find out if a student can join sets use the following number stories. Ask students to explain how they figured out each answer with words, pictures, or models.

Michael has three cookies. Carlos gives him two more cookies. How many cookies does Michael have now?

Gloria has large books and small books on her shelf. There are four large books and five small books. How many books are on Gloria's shelf?

Ten girls line up. Four boys line up. How many students are in the line?

Successful Strategies

To help build students' conceptual knowledge, provide them with models and meaningful situations. It is important that they visualize, manipulate, and talk about joining sets. Teachers do not need to be the sole providers of number stories. Students can and should create story problems as they learn what it means to join sets. Additionally, students need to understand that many sets can be joined. Misconceptions may occur for students if we only provide addition problems that have two addends.

> **Math Words to Use**
>
> **join, combine, add, addition, plus, sets, quantities, amounts**

Questions at Different *Levels of Cognitive Demand*

EASY

Recall: *What is four and three more?*

Comprehension: *How would you summarize what it means to join sets?*

Application: *How would you show four plus three?*

Analysis: *How are 2 + 3 and 4 + 1 alike?*

Evaluation: *What is the best way to join these sets?*

COMPLEX **Synthesis:** *How could you rearrange 5 + 2 + 5 + 3?*

Domino Dozen

A game designed to build the concept of joining sets

Materials:

- Set of Double-Six Dominoes

PLAYERS:
2

Directions:

1. Place dominoes face down so that dots cannot be seen. To start the game, flip one domino at random.
2. The first player flips a domino and joins the sets of dots on both dominoes.
3. If the total number of dots is a dozen (twelve), the player takes both dominoes. If the total number of dots is not a dozen, the player leaves the dominoes face up.
4. The second player flips one domino and looks for any face-up domino that could be combined with her domino to make a dozen dots. If a combination of twelve can be made, the player takes the dominoes. If a combination of twelve cannot be made the player leaves the dominoes face up.
5. Play continues until all dominoes have been flipped over.
6. The winner is the player with the most dominoes.

Content Differentiation:

Moving Back: Use cubes to represent the number of dots on the dominoes. Or focus on joining the sets of dots on individual dominoes, looking for combinations of six.

Moving Ahead: Write equations for each flip, for example. Or look for combinations of 18 using double-nine dominoes.

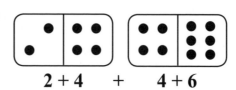

2 + 4   +   4 + 6

Number Line Proficiency

What is Number Line Proficiency?

Number line proficiency involves understanding the order and spacing of numbers assigned to points on a line. Even though every point on a number line has a unique real number (including fractions of fractions), students need to begin with number lines that have the counting by ones points labeled before moving to more complex labels. Number line proficiency includes knowing that on a horizontal number line, movement to the right represents addition and movement to the left represents subtraction. In addition to horizontal number lines, students should also have experiences with vertical number lines. Experiences with number lines that are separated into line segments, such as hundred charts and calendars, and circular number lines (technically not lines), such as analog clocks are also beneficial. Using number lines helps students build understanding of computation and number relationships.

Formative Assessment

To find out if a student has number line proficiency, show parts of various number lines and see if students can fill in the missing numbers. Notice if the student quickly identifies the correct missing numbers. Look for patterns in strategies and in errors.

Successful Strategies

For some students, the process of cutting out the rows of a hundred chart and taping the ends together helps them build understanding. They see how the number line is separated into line segments on the hundred chart. This same process can also be used with the calendar.

> ### Math Words to Use
>
> **number line, order,
> count, before, after**

Questions at Different *Levels of Cognitive Demand*

EASY

Recall: *What number comes next?*

Comprehension: *What are some examples of numbers that come before?*

Application: *How could you use the number line to show this math situation?*

Analysis: *What numbers go between other numbers on the number line?*

Evaluation: *Which number line works best? Why?*

Synthesis: *How would you design a number line that overlaps with another number line?*

COMPLEX

Number Line Fill Up

*A game designed to build the concept
of number line proficiency*

**PLAYERS:
2 OR MORE**

Materials:

- Number Line Fill Up template
  for each player
- Decahedron die (ten-sided, labeled 0-9)
  or 0-9 spinner *(see page 102)*

Directions:

1. Each player rolls the decahedron die (or spins the 0-9
   spinner) one time to find his start number.
2. Players decide where to write their start numbers on the
   Number Line Fill Up template.
3. All other rolls (or spins) are numbers shared by all players.
4. Each player records the new numbers one at a time. In this
   game, players are rolling (or spinning) one digit at a time to
   make 2-digit numbers in a counting by ones sequence. If a
   number cannot be used, the player waits for the next roll
   (or spin). Once a number is written, it cannot be moved.
5. The winner is the first player to complete an accurate
   number line chunk including four 2-digit numbers in order.

Content Differentiation:

Moving Back: Show values with base ten blocks or cubes
as students build the number line, or try the game using
single-digit numbers.

Moving Ahead: Add a third section to each number box and try
the game with 3-digit numbers, or try a skip counting sequence
on the number line.

Number Line Fill Up

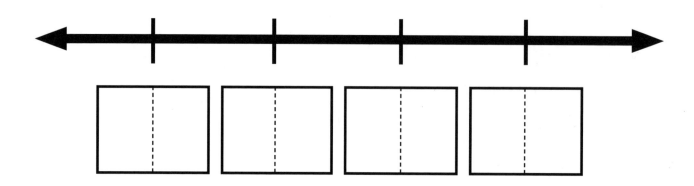

Number Line Fill Up

What is the Take Away Subtraction Concept?

Take away subtraction is one of three types of subtraction. Take away subtraction involves set removal. In number stories, a certain amount is removed, eaten, given, lost, hidden, or otherwise taken away. In a subtraction equation, the subtrahend is being subtracted from the minuend to find the difference. In the example $7 - 2 = 5$, 7 is the minuend, 2 is the subtrahend, and 5 is the difference. Students need many meaningful experiences to build conceptual understanding of take away subtraction.

Formative Assessment

To find out if a student understands take away subtraction, ask the student to tell a story that matches the following equation; $10 - 4 = 6$. Notice if the student uses words that represent take away subtraction. If the student is not successful, try a smaller equation such as $4 - 1 = 3$ and invite the student to use manipulatives to demonstrate as he tells the number story. If the student is successful with $10 - 4 = 6$, give a larger equation such as $25 - 6 = 19$ and invite the student to write the equation and tell a related number story.

Successful Strategies

The take away subtraction concept is best understood in context. Students need to engage in many types of take away situations to build conceptual understanding. Our goals are not for students to memorize vocabulary such as minuend and subtrahend. Instead we need to model these words as we teach the students the true meaning of take away subtraction.

> **Math Words to Use**
>
> subtract, subtraction, take away, minus sign, equation, minuend, subtrahend, difference

 ## Questions at Different *Levels of Cognitive Demand*

EASY

Recall: *What is eight take away three?*

Comprehension: *How would you explain take away subtraction?*

Application: *How would you use take away subtraction in this situation?*

Analysis: *Which number story represents take away subtraction?*

Evaluation: *Which type of subtraction best represents this math situation?*

Synthesis: *If you started with 6 more, how would that affect the difference?*

COMPLEX

Hungry Frog

A game designed to build the concept of take away subtraction

Materials:

PLAYERS: 2 OR MORE

- **Hungry Frog Game Board**
- **40 small counters**
- **Dice (two six-sided cubes labeled 1-6 with numerals)**

Directions:

1. Players place one counter on each fly on the game board.
2. The first player rolls both dice and decides which number she wants to use to represent how many flies Hungry Frog will eat. The player tells a number story about Hungry Frog eating flies, models the take away subtraction by taking away counters, and states the subtraction equation. For example, there are 40 flies. Hungry Frog eats three. Now there are 37 flies left, $40 - 3 = 37$.
3. The next player rolls the dice and chooses one of the numbers to be the subtrahend. The player tells the new subtraction story and states the equation. For example, $37 - 5 = 32$.
4. Players take turns rolling the dice, choosing a subtrahend, telling and modeling the associated number story, and stating the equation.
5. The winner is the player who has Hungry Frog eat the last fly. An exact number must be rolled to win.

Content Differentiation:

Moving Back: Use half of the game board and start with 20 flies.

Moving Ahead: Use mental math to play this game without counters or the game board. Tell different kinds of number stories.

Hungry Frog Game Board

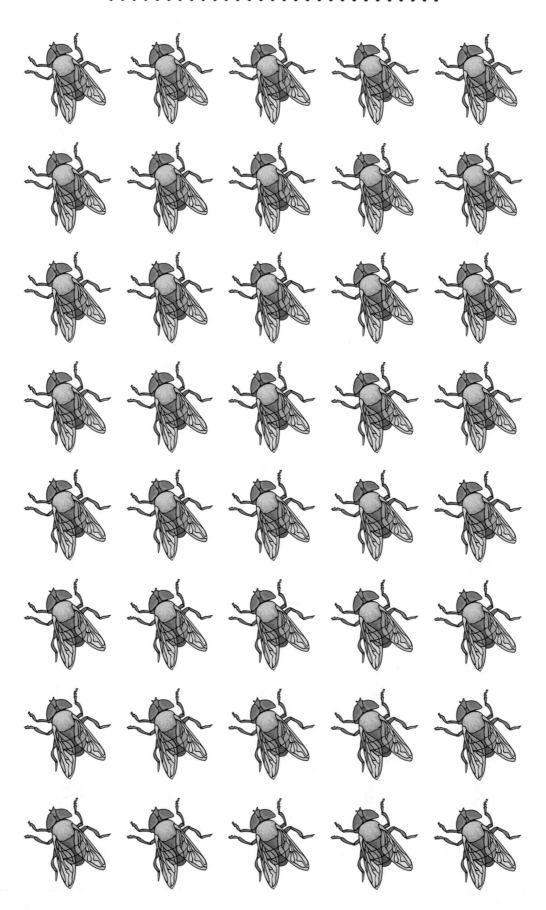

Math Intervention: Grades 3-5 • *Jennifer Taylor-Cox* • *© Eye On Education*

Missing Part Subtraction

What is Missing Part Subtraction?

Missing part subtraction is one of three types of subtraction. Missing part subtraction involves an unknown part of the whole. Either the subtrahend or the difference is unknown. For example, $10 - \square = 2$ or $10 - 8 = \square$. Missing part subtraction is often used to solve start unknown or change unknown addition problems. For example, $\square + 2 = 10$ or $8 + \square = 10$. When working with missing part subtraction, it is important that students use "subtract" rather than "take away" to more accurately describe the mathematics situation.

Formative Assessment

To find out if a student understands missing part subtraction, ask the student to solve the following number stories;

Melanie has 5 bracelets in her jewelry box. She puts some of the bracelets on her wrist. There are 2 bracelets left in her jewelry box. How many bracelets are on her wrist?

An apple tree has 11 beautiful apples. The wind blows 4 apples off the tree. How many apples are still on the tree?

Lenny bakes 24 cupcakes. He packs a lot of the cupcakes in a box and leaves 6 on the table. How many cupcakes are in the box?

Successful Strategies

To help students understand the concept of missing part subtraction use models to show the parts of the total. Color coding parts and arranging the parts in groups are helpful ways to highlight the parts within the whole set.

> **Math Words to Use**
>
> **subtract, subtraction, difference, minuend, subtrahend, minus sign, missing part**

Questions at Different *Levels of Cognitive Demand*

EASY

Recall: *What is 6 – 2?*

Comprehension: *How do you know that 10 – 3 = 7?*

Application: *Is there another number story that could go with this subtraction equation?*

Analysis: *Which number stories represent missing part subtraction?*

Evaluation: *What is the best way to model missing part subtraction?*

Synthesis: *How could you reorganize these facts to show a new pattern?*

COMPLEX

Broken Towers

*A game designed to build the concept
of missing part subtraction*

Materials:

- Linking cubes (20 for each player)

**PLAYERS:
3 OR MORE**

Directions:

1. The first player states a number (1-20).
2. All players build a tower using the stated number of cubes.
3. When the towers are completed, each player holds her tower under the table. The players break their towers into two parts.
4. One at a time, players show one part of their tower by placing it on the table. The other players count the cubes in the part of the tower that is showing and try to name how many cubes are in the missing part under the table.
5. The first player to name the correct number of cubes in the missing part of the tower earns one point. The player showing the tower can also earn one point by successfully stating the missing part subtraction equation.
6. After all players have shown their towers, the round is complete. A new number is given for the next round.
7. The winner is the player with the most points after five rounds.

Content Differentiation:

Moving Back: Build towers of ten or less.

Moving Ahead: Break towers into three parts.

CONCEPT:
Comparison Subtraction

What is Comparison Subtraction?

Comparison subtraction is one of three types of subtraction. In comparison subtraction, the focus is on the difference between quantities. Comparing means finding out how many more or how many less one number is compared to another number. As with missing part subtraction, comparison subtraction is not "take away." Finding the difference does not involve removal; therefore we should call it subtraction rather than "take away." Differences are reported in absolute values. This means that we do not need to teach students rules such as *the big number goes first when we subtract*. Instead, we can focus on teaching the concept of comparison subtraction because the difference between two numbers can be positive or negative.

Formative Assessment

To find out if a student understands comparison subtraction, give the student some numbers to compare. Ask the student to explain how he solved each problem.

What is the difference between 5 and 4?
What is the difference between 10 and 7?
What is the difference between 15 and 9?
What is the difference between 20 and 12?

If the student is successful, try numbers with greater differences. If the student is not successful, encourage the student to use objects to model the differences.

Successful Strategies

Comparison subtraction is difficult for many students. To help highlight differences between quantities, students can use manipulatives. Towers of cubes are especially helpful. When we ask the student to name the difference, we can discuss how many more are needed to make the towers even or equal.

> ### Math Words to Use
>
> **subtract, subtraction, compare, comparison, difference, subtrahend, minuend, minus sign**

Questions at Different *Levels of Cognitive Demand*

EASY

Recall: *What is the difference between 15 and 5?*

Comprehension: *How would you explain comparison subtraction?*

Application: *How would you show 12 – 4 with pictures?*

Analysis: *Which number stories represent comparison subtraction?*

Evaluation: *What is the best way to find the difference? Why is it best?*

Synthesis: *How would you design a new template for comparison subtraction?*

COMPLEX

Compare Bear

A game designed to build the concept of comparison subtraction

Materials:

PLAYERS: 2

- Number Mat for each player
- Two different colored bear counters for each player

Directions:

1. The first player drops the two bears onto the Number Mat. The player announces the two numbers that the bears land on (or are closest to) and states the difference. For example, if the bears land on 14 and 8, the player says, "The difference between 14 and 8 is 6."

2. The player also tells a comparison subtraction story. For example, "Blue Bear has 14 cookies. Red Bear has 8 cookies. Blue Bear has 6 more cookies than Red Bear."

3. The next player drops two bears on his number mat. The player announces the two numbers, states the difference, and tells a comparison subtraction story.

4. The player with the greater difference scores one point.

5. Players take turns dropping bears on their number mats, stating the difference, and telling the associated number stories.

6. The winner is the first player to score ten points.

Content Differentiation:

Moving Back: Use connecting cubes to show the numbers to help students see the differences.

Moving Ahead: Try the same game using a hundred chart as the number mat.

Number Mat

1	2	3	4	5
6	7	8	9	10
11	12	13	14	15
16	17	18	19	20

Adding and Subtracting Tens

What is the Adding and Subtracting Tens Concept?

Adding and subtracting tens builds fluency with number relationships and computation. When students understand the adding and subtracting tens concept, they are more apt to use mental math to solve problems and verify answers. Initially, students add and subtract tens to and from multiples of ten. Building on this idea, they learn to add and subtract tens to and from any number.

Formative Assessment

To find out if a student can add and subtract tens, ask the student to solve the following equations;

$20 + 10 =$
$40 - 10 =$
$50 + 30 =$
$70 - 20 =$
$65 + 10 =$
$82 - 10 =$
$38 + 40 =$
$97 - 30 =$

Ask the student to explain how he solved each problem. Analyze the student's proficiency through his accuracy, speed, and explanations.

Successful Strategies

One of the foundational concepts associated with adding and subtracting tens is rational counting by tens. Encourage students to skip count by tens beginning with zero and with numbers other than zero. To further help students understand the adding and subtracting tens concept, use base ten blocks or other manipulatives to model the computation.

> ### Math Words to Use
>
> **tens, add, addition, subtract, subtraction, minus sign, plus sign**

  ## Questions at Different *Levels of Cognitive Demand*

EASY

Recall: *What is 53 + 10?*

Comprehension: *How do you add ten to a number?*

Application: *How would you use 92 – 10 to solve 92 – 20?*

Analysis: *Which facts go together? Why?*

Evaluation: *How does skip counting help us add and subtract ten?*

Synthesis: *How could you use the adding and subtracting tens concept to add and subtract nines?*

COMPLEX

Hundred Chart Tic-Tac-Toe

*A game designed to build the concept
of adding and subtracting tens*

PLAYERS:
2

Materials:

- Markers or crayons
  (different color for each player)
- Paper

Directions:

1. Each player decides which color marker/crayon to use.
2. One player draws a tic-tac-toe board on the paper.
3. The first player writes a 2-digit number in one of the spaces.
4. The next player uses adding or subtracting ones or tens to write a related number in one of the spaces. The placement of numbers is relative to position on a hundred chart.
5. Players take turns filling in related numbers.
6. The winner is the first player to have three numbers in a horizontal, vertical, or diagonal row. For example;

Content Differentiation:

Moving Back: Use a hundred chart as a reference.

Moving Ahead: Make a tic-tac-toe board with more lines and try four in a row.

Adding Doubles and Near Doubles

What is the Adding Doubles and Near Doubles Concept?

There is something uniquely fascinating about doubles. Often students are keenly interested in doubles, which propels them to master these facts earlier than other facts. The smaller doubles (1+1, 2+2, 3+3, 4+4, 5+5) are often learned quickly. Larger doubles (6+6, 7+7, 8+8, 9+9) take more time for some students. To help students learn doubles, provide many experiences with doubling situations. Students also need to conceptually understand addition and the idea of "twice as many." When students own their doubles, meaning they do not need to count all or count on, they are ready to learn how to use this knowledge to solve near double addition problems. When teaching the near doubles concept, encourage students to identify the two doubles facts that the near double falls between and allow them to use plus one or minus one to solve the equation. For example, $7 + 8 = 15$ falls between $7 + 7 = 14$ and $8 + 8 = 16$. Rather than providing rules for students to follow, allow the students to decide which double they want to use to solve the near double problem. In this way, students learn more about number relationships. They know that they need to add one or subtract one because they understand the math involved.

Formative Assessment

To find out if a student can add doubles and near doubles, provide addition situations and ask them how they solved the problems. Ask the student to solve $5 + 5$ and see how quickly the student responds. Try other doubles ($1 + 1$ through $10 + 10$). Analyze the level of ownership by the accuracy and speed in which the student solves the problems. If the student owns her doubles, provide near doubles problems and ask students to explain how they solved the problems. Identify which doubles and near doubles the student owns and which the student does not own.

Successful Strategies

Teaching students to identify doubles and near doubles is the first step in ownership of these facts. Ask students to explain which two doubles facts "sandwich" the near doubles fact. Use manipulatives (towers of cubes or stacks of counters) to model one more and one less. Write out the facts in order so that students can see the patterns. As students gain ownership of doubles and near doubles, we need to encourage them to use this knowledge with related subtraction facts.

> ## Math Words to Use
>
> **doubles, twice as many,
> add, addition, facts, sum,
> near doubles, one more,
> one less**

 ## Questions at Different *Levels of Cognitive Demand*

 EASY

Recall: *What is 4 + 4?*

Comprehension: *How would you explain double?*

Application: *How could you use 6 + 6 to solve 6 + 7?*

Analysis: *Why is 5 + 5 similar to 10 + 10?*

Evaluation: *How would you help someone else solve 7 + 8?*

Synthesis: *What if you were to invent a new way to organize the doubles facts?*

COMPLEX

X Marks the Spot

A game designed to build the concept of adding doubles and near doubles

PLAYERS: 2

Materials:

- 0-9 Number Cards or 0-9 Number Tiles in a paper cup
- X Marks the Spot Game Boards
- Two highlighters or light markers (different colors)

Directions:

1. Players decide which color highlighter each person will use.
2. Without looking into the cup, the first player chooses a number. The player doubles the number and looks for the sum on the game board.
3. The player marks the sum with a dot using the highlighter to "hold" the spot and places the number back into the cup.
4. The next player chooses a number, doubles the number and looks for the sum on the game board. The player can mark the sum with a dot to hold it OR the player can "claim" any sum that is currently being held with a dot.
5. If the player claims a held sum, the highlighter is used to draw X on the sum.
6. Players take turns choosing numbers, doubling, and holding or claiming sums. *NOTE: All sums must be held before they are claimed. Held sums can be claimed by any player.*
7. The winner is the first player to have four claimed sums (Xs) in a row (horizontal, vertical, or diagonal).

Content Differentiation:

Moving Back: Play the game without holding sums prior to claiming sums.

Moving Ahead: Play the same game using Near Doubles. The near double is one more or one less than the closest double.

0-9 Number Cards

. . . .

0	1	2	3	4
5	6	7	8	9

X Marks the Spot Game Board for Doubles

X Marks the Spot Game Board for Near Doubles

Fact Families—Addition and Subtraction

 ## What are Addition and Subtraction Fact Families?

Fact families for addition and subtraction are facts that are directly related. In a fact family, there are two addition problems and two subtraction problems. The addition facts are manifestations of the commutative property. The subtraction facts are inverse operations of the addition facts.

 ## Formative Assessment

To find out if a student understands addition and subtraction fact families, provide the following incomplete fact family and ask the student which fact is missing from the family.

$8 + 4 = 12$
$12 - 4 = 8$
$12 - 8 = 4$

If the student is not successful, try a smaller fact family. If the student is successful, ask her to generate all of the facts in the 7, 8, 15 fact family.

Successful Strategies

Some students struggle with fact families. One of the ways to help these students is to go back to the parts and total concept. Focusing on the parts of a given total encourages students to think about the related addition and subtraction facts. Additionally, help student see why doubles produce identical facts.

Math Words to Use

addition, subtraction, equation, facts, fact families

Questions at Different *Levels of Cognitive Demand*

EASY

Recall: *What is 5 + 2? What is 2 + 5?*

Comprehension: *How would you explain fact families?*

Application: *How would you show the fact family of 6, 7, 13?*

Analysis: *What relationship do you see between 8 + 9 and 17 − 9?*

Evaluation: *What advice would you give to someone who does not understand fact families?*

Synthesis: *Is it possible to have a fact family for this equation 2 + 3 + 4 = 9?*

COMPLEX

Funny Bunny

A game designed to build the concept
of addition and subtraction fact families

Materials:

PLAYERS: 2

- Funny Bunny Resource Pages
- Straws
- Tape

Directions:

1. Cut out bunnies and tape each bunny on a straw.
2. Place all bunny puppets face down on the table.
3. The first player chooses a bunny and folds back one of the bunny's ears.
4. The other player names the hidden number on the bunny's ear. The player receives one point for each fact in the fact family that is named correctly.
5. Players take turns choosing bunnies, folding ears, and naming the facts in the fact family.
6. The first player to reach 20 or more points is the winner.

Content Differentiation:

Moving Back: Look at the bunny with both ears up and name the facts in the fact family.

Moving Ahead: Use the blank bunnies to make different fact families.

Funny Bunny Resource Page

Funny Bunny Resource Page

Funny Bunny Resource Page

What is the Partial Sums Concept?

The partial sums concept is an addition strategy that involves combining addends into workable clusters. The traditional algorithm for addition involves following procedures, such as *aligning digits in columns* and *always starting with the ones*. The rules of the traditional algorithm are meaningless for many students. They cannot remember what to do because they do not understand the math. Alternative algorithms such as partial sums build conceptual understanding. With partial sums, it does not matter if columns are aligned or if the student starts with the ones or not. There is no need to "carry." For example, $37 + 48 = 70 + 15$. In this situation, the tens are clustered (70 is a partial sum) and the ones are clustered (15 is a partial sum). The partial sums are easily combined into 85. The idea with partial sums is to cluster the addends in a way that invites mental math.

Formative Assessment

To find out if a student understands the partial sums concept, ask the student to solve the following equations;

$23 + 42 =$	$26 + 23 =$	$31 + 39 =$
$68 + 12 =$	$57 + 38 =$	$76 + 17 =$

Ask the student to explain how she solves each problem. If the student uses the traditional algorithm (successfully or not successfully), ask the student if she knows another way to solve the equations. Invite the student to try the problems without aligning the digits in columns and without starting with the ones.

Successful Strategies

Some of the reasons students struggle with the traditional algorithm include the phrases that they have heard. For example, many people say things like, "Carry the one," when they are actually regrouping a ten. Because the math language is not accurate, the students develop misconceptions. The partial sums concept is embedded in place value and conceptual understanding, which help remedy algorithmic misconceptions. Even if students successfully use the traditional algorithm, learning the partial sums concept invites students to strengthen conceptual understanding, increase mental math capacity, and improve flexibility and fluency.

> ### Math Words to Use
>
> **partial, part, sum,**
> **addition, add, strategy,**
> **equation, equal**

 ## Questions at Different *Levels of Cognitive Demand*

EASY

Recall: *What is 25 + 15?*

Comprehension: *How did you solve the problem?*

Application: *What picture could you draw to show the partial sums?*

Analysis: *How would you compare the partial sums?*

Evaluation: *What is good about the partial sums concept?*

Synthesis: *How would you design a template for reordering partial sums?*

COMPLEX

Race to the Top

A game designed to build the concept of partial sums

PLAYERS: 2 OR 3

Materials:

- **Race to the Top Game Board**
- **Four sets of 0-9 Number Cards**
- **Two Pawns**

Directions:

1. **Players shuffle each set of number cards and place cards face down in a pile near each of the template boxes on the game board.**
2. **Players decide the ladder each person will use and place a pawn at the bottom of this ladder.**
3. **The player on the left flips over the top card in the first pile and places it in the first box. He flips over the top card in the second pile and places it in the second box.**
4. **The player on the right does the same with the third and fourth piles of cards and boxes.**
5. **Players read the equation. The goal is not to name the sum. Rather, the goal is to name the partial sums. For example, $36 + 27 = 50 + 13$.**
6. **The first player to name the correct partial sums moves his pawn one step up the ladder.** *NOTE: Player 3 is the "judge" determining which player is first to name the partial sums.*
7. **Play continues until the winning player reaches the top of the ladder.** *NOTE: Players can take turns being first to flip cards.*

Content Differentiation:

Moving Back: **Use base ten blocks or other manipulatives to show the partial sums.**

Moving Ahead: **Try this game with 3-digit numbers.**

Race to the Top Game Board

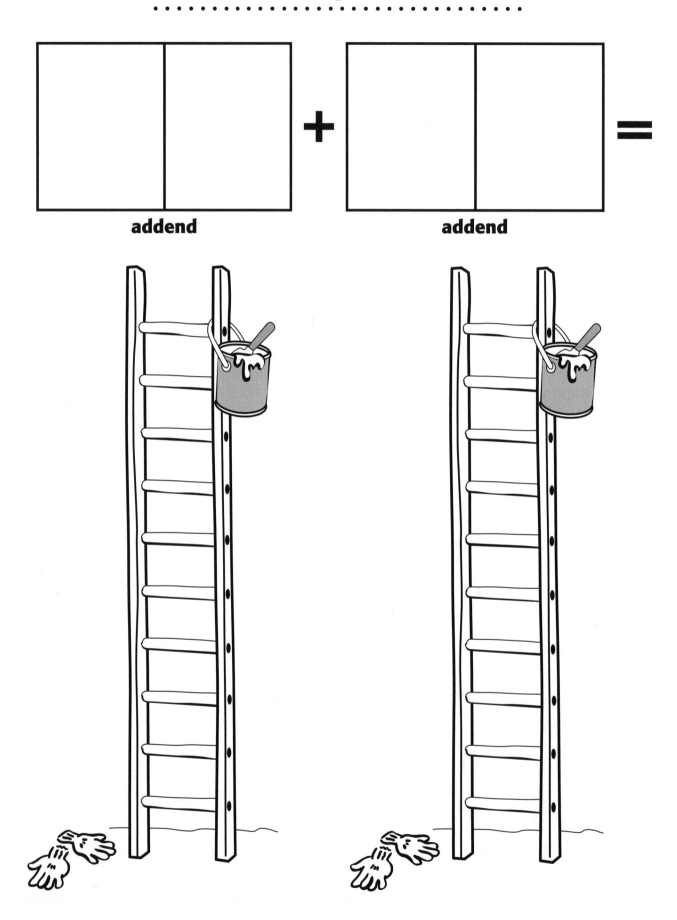

addend $+$ addend $=$

Math Intervention: Grades 3-5 • *Jennifer Taylor-Cox* • *© Eye On Education*

0-9 Number Cards

What is the Partial Differences Concept?

The partial differences concept is a subtraction strategy that involves combining differences into workable clusters. Like partial sums, this concept serves as an alternative to the traditional algorithm. Instead of following rules that are meaningless to some students, the students using the partial differences strategy do not have to *align columns, start with the ones*, or *cross out*. Instead, students find the difference between the tens, then find the difference between the ones, and combine these differences. For example, $57 - 26 = (50 - 20) + (7 - 6)$. In this situation, the difference between the tens is 30 and the difference between the ones is 1. These partial differences are combined into $30 + 1 = 31$. The partial differences concept is also an effective strategy when a subtraction situation involves regrouping. For example, $84 - 36 = (80 - 30) + (4 - 6)$. In this situation, the difference between the tens is 50 and the difference between the ones is -2. These partial differences are combined into $50 - 2 = 48$.

 ## Formative Assessment

To find out if a student understands partial differences, ask the student to solve the following equations;

$37 - 12 =$	$45 - 23 =$	$57 - 34 =$
$64 - 25 =$	$52 - 36 =$	$70 - 28 =$

Ask the student to explain how she solves each problem. If the student uses the traditional algorithm (successfully or not successfully), ask the student if she knows another way to solve the equations. Encourage the student to try the problems without aligning the digits in columns, without starting with the ones, and without crossing out.

Successful Strategies

Using number lines that include negative numbers helps students understand how to find the partial differences when the ones digit value of the minuend is greater than the ones digit value of the subtrahend. It also helps us focus on mathematical truths. It really is a lie when we tell students *you cannot take 6 from 4*. You can take 6 from 4. The result is -2. When the partial differences are combined, you just subtract without the need to memorize rules about adding positive and negative numbers. As with partial sums, even if students successfully use the traditional algorithm, learning the partial differences concept strengthens their conceptual understanding, increases mental math capacity, and improves flexibility and fluency.

> ### Math Words to Use
>
> **partial, part, difference, subtract, subtraction, strategy, equation, equal, subtrahend, minuend**

Questions at Different *Levels of Cognitive Demand*

EASY

Recall: *What is 46 – 21?*

Comprehension: *How did you solve the problem?*

Application: *What picture could you draw to show partial differences?*

Analysis: *How would you compare the partial differences?*

Evaluation: *What is helpful about the partial differences concept?*

Synthesis: *What if the partial differences were half as many?*

COMPLEX

Race to the Bottom

A game designed to build the concept of partial differences

PLAYERS: 2 OR 3

Materials:

- **Two sets of 0-9 Number Cards** *(see page 63)*
- **One set of 5-9 Number Cards**
- **One set of 1-4 Number Cards**
- **Race to the Bottom Game Board**
- **Number Line and two pawns**

Directions:

1. **Players shuffle each set of number cards and place the cards face down in a pile near each of the template boxes on the game board.** *NOTE: The 5-9 cards are used for the tens digit of the minuend. The 1-4 cards are used for the tens digit of the subtrahend.*
2. **Players decide the ladder each person will use and place a pawn at the top of this ladder.**
3. **The player on the left flips over the top card in the first pile and places it in the first box. He flips over the top card in the second pile and places it in the second box.**
4. **The player on the right does the same with the third and fourth piles of cards and boxes.**
5. **Players read the equation. The goal is not to name the difference. Rather, the goal is to name the partial differences, for example, $63 - 27 = 40 - 4$. Use number line as needed.**
6. **The first player to name the correct partial differences moves his pawn one step down the ladder. Play continues until the winning player reaches the bottom of his ladder.** *NOTE: Player 3 is the "judge" determining which player is first to name the partial differences.*

Content Differentiation:

Moving Back: Use base ten blocks or other manipulatives to show the partial differences.

Moving Ahead: Try this game with 3-digit numbers.

Race to the Bottom Game Board

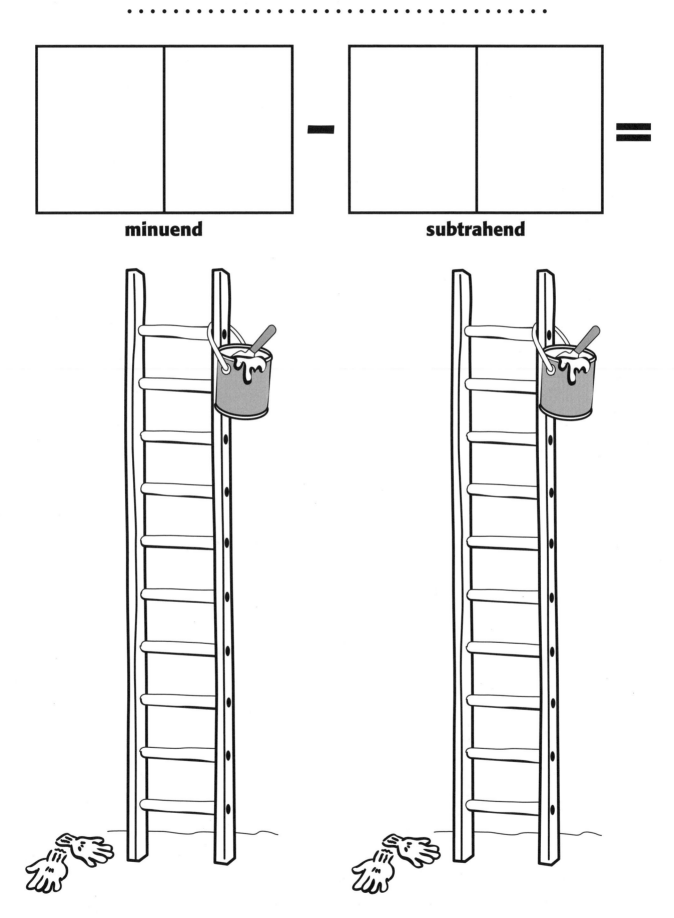

minuend   —   subtrahend   =

Number Line

· · · · · · · · · · · · · · ·

Near Tens for Addition and Subtraction

 ## What is the Near Tens Concept?

The near tens concept involves adjusting numbers based on their proximity to ten. The near tens concept can be used in addition, for example, $57 + 9 = 57 + 10 - 1$ or $57 + 8 = 57 + 10 - 2$. The near tens concept can also be used in subtraction, for example $83 - 9 = 83 - 10 + 1$ or $83 - 8 = 83 - 10 + 2$. When students use the near tens concept, they apply the kind of flexibility with numbers that is needed for mental math and deep conceptual understanding.

 ## Formative Assessment

To find out if a student understands the near tens concept, ask the student to solve the following equations;

$48 + 10 =$	$56 + 20 =$
$73 - 10 =$	$67 - 30 =$
$53 + 9 =$	$47 + 29 =$
$64 - 9 =$	$93 - 49 =$
$26 + 8 =$	$44 + 28 =$
$56 - 8 =$	$77 - 38 =$

Ask students to explain how they solve each problem. If the student uses the traditional algorithm (successfully or not successfully), ask the student if she knows another way to solve the equations. Invite the student to try the problems using what they know about adding and subtracting tens.

Successful Strategies

To be successful with the near tens concept, it is essential that students have ownership of plus or minus ten. The near tens concept builds upon what students know about adding and subtracting tens. For many students, using the hundred chart helps them to see and apply the near tens concept.

> ### Math Words to Use
>
> **near ten, add, addition, subtract, subtraction, adjust, compensate**

 ## Questions at Different *Levels of Cognitive Demand*

EASY

Recall: *What is 97 – 10 ?*

Comprehension: *How could you use a near ten to solve 43 + 29?*

Application: *How would you show the near tens concept with manipulatives?*

Analysis: *Which problems work better with the near tens concept?*

Evaluation: *When is it not a good plan to use the near tens concept?*

Synthesis: *How would you teach the near tens concept to someone who did not know it?*

COMPLEX

Drop It

A game designed to build the concept of near tens

Materials:

- **Die (labeled 18, 28, 39, 49, 40, 50)**
- **Plus/Minus Spinner, paper clip and pencil**
- **Drop It Hundred Chart**
- **Chip or counter**

PLAYERS: 2

Directions:

1. The first player spins the spinner to find out if he will add or subtract.
2. The first player drops the chip/counter on the hundred chart to find one of the numbers in his equation and rolls the die to find the other number in the equation. *NOTE: The chip/counter is dropped on the 1-50 section (shaded) for addition and the 51-100 section (not shaded) for subtraction. This number serves as the first addend or the minuend. The number on the die serves as the second addend or the subtrahend.* **For example, 74 – 39 = ? The player touches 74 on the hundred chart, moves his finger up four rows of ten (– 40) and forward one space to the right (+ 1). The player describes the near tens situation, for example, 74 – 39 = 74 – 40 + 1.**
3. The sum/difference is the player's positive score for the round.
4. The next player spins the spinner, drops the chip/counter, rolls the die, models, and describes the near tens equation.
5. Players add their scores from each round. The winning player is the player with the highest score after 10 rounds.

Content Differentiation:

Moving Back: **Try the game with a die labeled 8, 8, 9, 9, 10, 10.**

Moving Ahead: **Try the game with a die labeled 38, 48, 58, 69, 79, 89 using a two-hundred chart.**

Plus/Minus Spinner

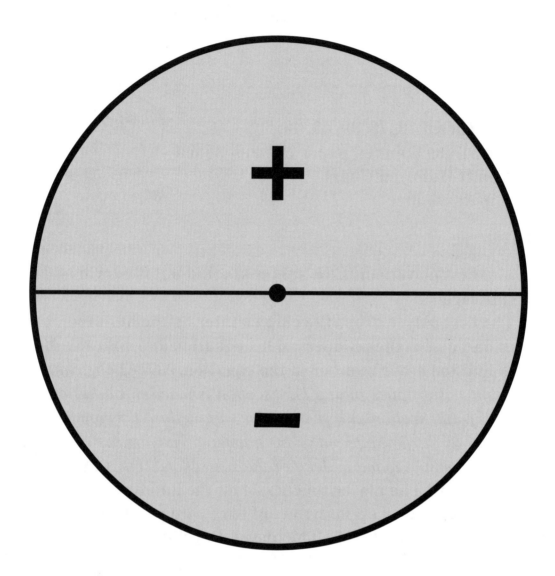

To use the spinner, place a paper clip in the center. Place pencil point through the paper clip at the center of the spinner. Holding the pencil securely with one hand, spin the paper clip with the other hand.

Drop It Hundred Chart

1	2	3	4	5	6	7	8	9	10
11	12	13	14	15	16	17	18	19	20
21	22	23	24	25	26	27	28	29	30
31	32	33	34	35	36	37	38	39	40
41	42	43	44	45	46	47	48	49	50
51	52	53	54	55	56	57	58	59	60
61	62	63	64	65	66	67	68	69	70
71	72	73	74	75	76	77	78	79	80
81	82	83	84	85	86	87	88	89	90
91	92	93	94	95	96	97	98	99	100

Equal Differences

What is the Equal Difference Concept?

The equal difference concept is a subtraction strategy based on the idea that different subtraction expressions can have the same difference. The focus is on the value between numbers, for example, $76 - 29 = 77 - 30$. By adding one to the subtrahend and one to the minuend, we create an expression that is more easily solved. In some situations, it makes sense to add two to the subtrahend and the minuend, for example, $52 - 28 = 54 - 30$. In some situations, we may subtract from the subtrahend and the minuend to create a new expression with the same difference. For example, $68 - 41 = 67 - 40$ or $96 - 82 = 94 - 80$. Understanding how to mentally create expressions with the same differences helps students learn to build flexibility and fluency with numbers and operations.

Formative Assessment

To find out if a student understands the equal difference concept, ask the student if the following equations are true or not;

$54 - 29 = 55 - 30$
$76 - 48 = 78 - 50$
$87 - 34 = 90 - 31$
$81 - 34 = 80 - 33$

Ask the student to explain why these equations are true or not true (the third equation is NOT true). Notice if the student solves each side of the equation to verify the answer or if the student uses the equal difference concept.

Successful Strategies

The equal difference concept is applicable in any given subtraction equation, but it is most efficient when the created expression invites mental math. For example, $73 - 25 = 74 - 26$. The created expression does not necessarily increase opportunities for mental math. It is beneficial for students to think about when to use the equal difference concept and when it may be better to use a different concept.

> ## Math Words to Use
>
> **equal, difference, subtract, subtraction, add, addition, expression, equation**

 # Questions at Different *Levels of Cognitive Demand*

EASY

Recall: *What is the difference between 52 and 39?*

Comprehension: *Which examples could you give of the equal difference concept?*

Application: *How would you show the equal difference concept on a number line?*

Analysis: *How are these expressions related?*

Evaluation: *Which problems work best with the equal difference concept?*

Synthesis: *What if you were to create a new way to record twice the difference?*

COMPLEX

All Strung Out

A game designed to build the concept of equal difference

Materials:

- **Number Cards (50-98)**
- **One Subtrahend Spinner (+2 or +1 or –1)**
- **Paper clip and pencil**
- **Number line (1-100)** *NOTE: If number line is not available, cut apart the rows of a hundred chart and tape the ends together.*
- **String/yarn, scissors**

PLAYERS: 2 OR MORE

Directions:

1. Shuffle the number cards and place face-down in a pile. The first player draws a card. This number will be the minuend.
2. The first player spins the spinner to find the subtrahend for the subtraction expression. This player cuts a piece of string that shows the difference (distance between the minuend and the subtrahend). The player moves the string two numbers to the right (when using the +2 spinner) and describes the equal difference equation using the term "is the same as." For example, 86 – 28 *is the same as* 88 – 30.
3. If the player accurately models and describes the equal difference equation, the player keeps the string.
4. Players take turns drawing number cards, spinning, modeling, and describing the equal difference expressions.
5. After each player has five turns, all players line up their pieces of string, and compare their total lengths. The winner is the player with the most string.

Content Differentiation:

Moving Back: Use the +1 spinner (move string <u>one</u> number to the right).

Moving Ahead: Use the –1 spinner (move string <u>one</u> number to the left) or make your own spinner.

All Strung Out Number Cards

50	**51**	**52**	**53**	**54**
55	**56**	**57**	**58**	**59**
60	**61**	**62**	**63**	**64**
65	**66**	**67**	**68**	**69**
70	**71**	**72**	**73**	**74**

All Strung Out Number Cards

75	**76**	**77**	**78**	**79**
80	**81**	**82**	**83**	**84**
85	**86**	**87**	**88**	**89**
90	**91**	**92**	**93**	**94**
95	**96**	**97**	**98**	

Subtrahend Spinner Options

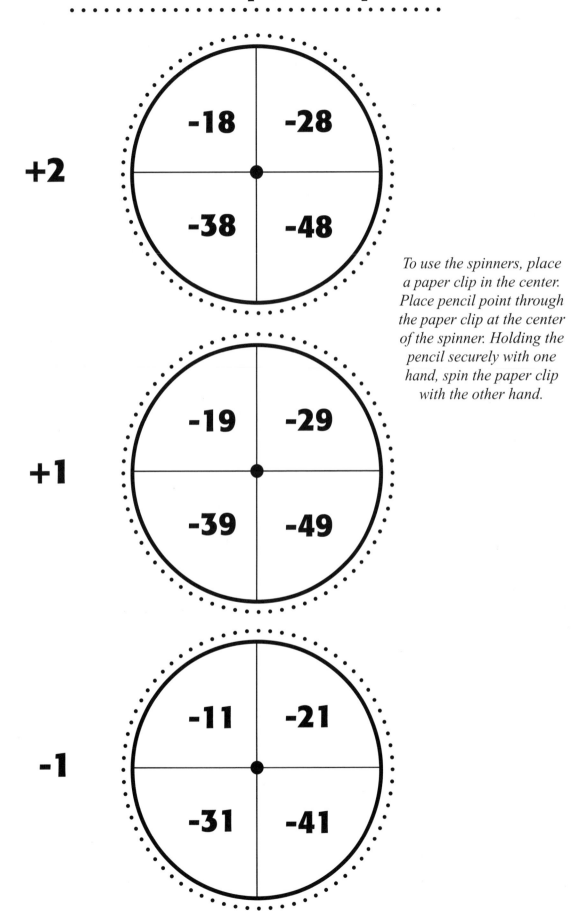

+2

| -18 | -28 |
| -38 | -48 |

To use the spinners, place a paper clip in the center. Place pencil point through the paper clip at the center of the spinner. Holding the pencil securely with one hand, spin the paper clip with the other hand.

+1

| -19 | -29 |
| -39 | -49 |

-1

| -11 | -21 |
| -31 | -41 |

CHAPTER

Multiplication and Division Concepts

Repeated Addition Multiplication

Repeated Subtraction Division

Fair Shares Division

Rectangular Arrays for Multiplication and Division

Multiplying and Dividing by Ten

Perfect Squares and Near Squares

Near Tens for Multiplication

Fact Families—Multiplication and Division

Partial Products

Partial Quotients

Equal Products

Repeated Addition Multiplication

 ## What is the Repeated Addition Multiplication Concept?

When we multiply, the result is the total number referred to as the product. In multiplication, we combine a certain number of groups which is the multiplier. Each group has the same quantity which is the multiplicand. Because addition and multiplication are interrelated operations, we obtain the same results by repeated addition. For example, 3 x 5 = 5 + 5 + 5. There are 3 groups of 5. Some students are encouraged to memorize multiplication facts before they understand the concept of multiplication. The result is inconsistent surface knowledge. Working with repeated addition as a way to understand multiplication helps students to build foundations necessary to develop permanent ownership of multiplication facts.

 ## Formative Assessment

To find out if a student understands repeated addition multiplication, give the student the following repeated addition equations and ask the student to give the related multiplication equation.

3 + 3 + 3 + 3 =   8 + 8 + 8 =

If the student is successful, provide the following multiplication equations and ask the student to give the related repeated addition equations.

7 x 4 =   6 x 9 =

If the student is not successful with either set of problems, try groups of two, five, or ten. If the student is successful with both sets of problems, try more complex problems.

Successful Strategies

When working with the repeated addition multiplication concept, it is often beneficial to model the groups with manipulatives or show the groups with pictures. It is also helpful to put the mathematical situations in context. For example, $4 + 4 + 4$ can be placed in the context of three cars with four people in each car. Students can draw pictures of the cars and people or use manipulatives to show the groups of people. In addition, it is beneficial to begin making the connection to multiplication by using the phrase, "groups of." Saying, "There are 3 groups of 4," is a helpful bridge from $4 + 4 + 4$ to 3×4. The word "times" may cause confusion for students. Beginning with "groups of" helps students to understand the concept and progress to other ways to communicate the concept such as using the word "times."

Math Words to Use

repeat, repeated, addition,
add, multiply, multiplication,
groups, sets, multiplier,
multiplicand, product

 ## Questions at Different *Levels of Cognitive Demand*

EASY

Recall: *What is 2 + 2 + 2 + 2 + 2?*

Comprehension: *How do know that 5 + 5 + 5 + 5 = 20?*

Application: *How would you illustrate 6 groups of 3?*

Analysis: *How does skip counting connect to repeated addition?*

Evaluation: *Why is repeated addition a multiplication concept?*

Synthesis: *What kind of diagram could you create to show repeated addition?*

COMPLEX

Cakes and Candles

*A game designed to build the concept
of repeated addition multiplication*

**PLAYERS:
2 OR MORE**

Materials:

- One white die (labeled 1-6 with numerals)
- One red die (labeled 1-6 with numerals)
- Paper and pencil (or dry erase board and marker) for each player

Directions:

1. The first player rolls the dice. The white die represents the cakes. The red die represents the candles on each cake.
2. Players race to draw the number of cakes and the number of candles on each cake. For example, if the number on the white die is 3 and the number on the red die is 2, the illustration may look like this...

3. The first player to complete the picture and call out the total number of candles (product) scores two points.
4. If the player who rolled the dice can state the "groups of" equation, she earns one point. For example, "3 groups of 2 equal 6."
5. Players continue taking turns rolling, illustrating, calling out the product, and giving equations.
6. The winner is the first player to score 20 or greater.

Content Differentiation:

Moving Back: Use dice labeled 1, 1, 2, 2, 3, 3 with numerals.

Moving Ahead: Use decahedron dice (labeled 0-9) or 0-9 spinner *(see page 102)*.

Repeated Subtraction Division

 What is the Repeated Subtraction Division Concept?

When we divide, we find the number of times a number is divisible; the result is the quotient. In division, the number that is divided is called the dividend. The number that divides the dividend is called the divisor. Because subtraction and division are interrelated operations, we obtain the same results by repeated subtraction. For example, $15 \div 3$ can be solved by subtracting. Groups of 3 are subtracted from the dividend until zero is reached. We keep track of how many groups are subtracted to find the quotient. Some students are encouraged to memorize division facts before they understand the concept of division. Working with repeated subtraction as a way to understand division builds necessary foundations for students.

 Formative Assessment

To find out if a student understands repeated subtraction division, give the student the following repeated subtraction equations and ask the student to give the related division equation.

$16 - 4 - 4 - 4 - 4 =$ $21 - 7 - 7 - 7 =$

If the student is successful, provide the following division equations and ask the student to give the related repeated subtraction equations.

$35 \div 5 =$ $56 \div 8 =$

If the student is not successful with either set of problems, try subtracting groups of two, five, or ten. If the student is successful with both sets of problems, try more complex problems.

Successful Strategies

When working with the repeated subtraction division concept, it is often beneficial to model the subtraction of groups with manipulatives or to show the subtraction of groups with pictures. It is also helpful to put the mathematical situations in context. For example, $12 - 4 - 4 - 4$ can be placed in the context of twelve cookies placed in sets of four on plates. Students can draw pictures of the plates and cookies or use manipulatives to show the sets of cookies. It is also beneficial to begin making the connection to division by continually asking, "How many groups have been subtracted?" and "Are there enough left to subtract another group?" These questions help students to strengthen their understanding of division.

Math Words to Use
repeat, repeated, subtraction, subtract, divide, division, groups, sets, dividend, divisor, quotient

 ## Questions at Different *Levels of Cognitive Demand*

EASY

Recall: *What is $8 - 2 - 2 - 2 - 2$?*

Comprehension: *How do know that $15 - 5 - 5 - 5 = 0$?*

Application: *How could you use repeated subtraction to solve $20 \div 4$?*

Analysis: *How would you compare this repeated subtraction problem with another?*

Evaluation: *What would you recommend to help someone learn repeated subtraction?*

Synthesis: *What if there are leftovers after the repeated subtraction?*

COMPLEX

Cookies for My Friends

A game designed to build the concept of repeated subtraction division

PLAYERS: 3 OR MORE

Materials:

- 10 paper plates
- 100 counting chips
- Cookie Cards cut apart and placed in a cup
- Paper and pencil (or dry erase board & marker) for each player

Directions:

1. The first player chooses a random cookie card from the cup. The player gathers this many counting chips to represent cookies.

2. The player reads how many cookies each friend gets and begins subtracting out sets of cookies represented by chips. The player places sets of cookies on plates. Other players consider how many friends will share the cookies/how many plates will be used/how many times the divisor can be subtracted. The other players race to draw a picture of what the model will look like when complete.

3. The first person who completes an accurate illustration scores one point. *NOTE: The player modeling the repeated subtraction with chips and plates does not try to score.*

4. Players take turns choosing cookie cards, modeling different repeated subtraction scenarios, and illustrating the models.

5. The winner is the first player to earn ten points.

Content Differentiation:

Moving Back: Use first five rows of cookie cards.

Moving Ahead: Make your own cookie cards. Try remainders.

Cookie Cards
. . . .

1 cookie Each friend gets 1 cookie	**2 cookies** Each friend gets 1 cookie	**3 cookies** Each friend gets 3 cookies	**4 cookies** Each friend gets 1 cookie	**5 cookies** Each friend gets 5 cookies
6 cookies Each friend gets 1 cookie	**7 cookies** Each friend gets 7 cookies	**8 cookies** Each friend gets 1 cookie	**9 cookies** Each friend gets 9 cookies	**10 cookies** Each friend gets 1 cookie
4 cookies Each friend gets 2 cookies	**6 cookies** Each friend gets 3 cookies	**8 cookies** Each friend gets 2 cookies	**10 cookies** Each friend gets 5 cookies	**12 cookies** Each friend gets 6 cookies
14 cookies Each friend gets 2 cookies	**16 cookies** Each friend gets 8 cookies	**18 cookies** Each friend gets 2 cookies	**20 cookies** Each friend gets 10 cookies	**9 cookies** Each friend gets 3 cookies
12 cookies Each friend gets 3 cookies	**15 cookies** Each friend gets 5 cookies	**18 cookies** Each friend gets 3 cookies	**21 cookies** Each friend gets 7 cookies	**24 cookies** Each friend gets 3 cookies
27 cookies Each friend gets 9 cookies	**30 cookies** Each friend gets 3 cookies	**16 cookies** Each friend gets 4 cookies	**20 cookies** Each friend gets 4 cookies	**24 cookies** Each friend gets 6 cookies
28 cookies Each friend gets 4 cookies	**32 cookies** Each friend gets 8 cookies	**36 cookies** Each friend gets 4 cookies	**40 cookies** Each friend gets 10 cookies	**25 cookies** Each friend gets 5 cookies
30 cookies Each friend gets 5 cookies	**35 cookies** Each friend gets 7 cookies	**40 cookies** Each friend gets 5 cookies	**45 cookies** Each friend gets 9 cookies	**50 cookies** Each friend gets 5 cookies
36 cookies Each friend gets 6 cookies	**42 cookies** Each friend gets 7 cookies	**48 cookies** Each friend gets 6 cookies	**54 cookies** Each friend gets 9 cookies	**60 cookies** Each friend gets 6 cookies
49 cookies Each friend gets 7 cookies	**56 cookies** Each friend gets 8 cookies	**63 cookies** Each friend gets 7 cookies	**70 cookies** Each friend gets 10 cookies	**64 cookies** Each friend gets 8 cookies
72 cookies Each friend gets 8 cookies	**80 cookies** Each friend gets 10 cookies	**81 cookies** Each friend gets 9 cookies	**90 cookies** Each friend gets 9 cookies	**100 cookies** Each friend gets 10 cookies

Fair Shares Division

What is the Fair Shares Division Concept?

The fair shares concept is similar to the repeated subtraction concept because it is division. The fair shares concept is different from the repeated subtraction concept because the number of groups is known but the amount in each group is unknown. With repeated subtraction the number in each group is known but the number of groups is unknown. When students work with fair shares they are partitioning or splitting up the dividend into a specific number of groups. When students partition a given quantity, they distribute equal amounts, one at a time, much like when a person deals out cards.

Formative Assessment

To find out if a student understands fair shares division, give the student a set of 48 counters and explain that the student will use counters to model the problem.

There are 48 pieces of candy. There are four boxes. How many pieces of candy go inside each box?

Notice if and how the student partitions the dividend. If the student is not successful, try a similar story with easier numbers. If the student is successful try a similar story using numbers that result in a remainder situation.

Successful Strategies

Students benefit from engaging in fair shares division by actually partitioning, not just watching someone partition. This active learning helps students to build background experiences and solidify their learning. Likewise, an illustration of fair shares division should not replace actual experiences. However, an illustration following the partitioning experience serves as a beneficial way to communicate the mathematics. To make the division connections while students are partitioning teachers should ask, "How many are in each group so far?" and "How many more do you think each group will get?" These questions and others help students strengthen their understanding of division.

> ### Math Words to Use
>
> **fair shares, groups, sets, remainder, divide, division, dividend, divisor, quotient**

 Questions at Different *Levels of Cognitive Demand*

EASY

Recall: *What is the divisor?*

Comprehension: *How would you describe fair shares division?*

Application: *When would you use fair shares to solve a problem?*

Analysis: *How would you compare fair shares to repeated subtraction?*

Evaluation: *In your judgement, is the fair shares concept helpful? Why?*

Synthesis: *What kind of song could you create about fair shares division?*

COMPLEX

Piggy Banks

*A game designed to build the concept
of fair shares division*

PLAYERS: 2 OR MORE

Materials:

- 100 pennies
- Hundred chart
- Scissors
- Cup
- 12 Piggy Banks

Directions:

1. Cut apart the numbers in the hundred chart. Place the numbers 1-100 in a cup.
2. The first player chooses one random number from the cup. This number is used as the dividend. The player gathers pennies to represent the dividend. The player then decides how many piggy banks to use to try to have fair shares. The player lays out the piggy banks.
3. The player then distributes the pennies in equal amounts, one at a time to each bank.
4. If the player distributes fair shares, meaning there are no left over pennies, the player earns 1 point for each piggy bank used. If there is a remainder, no points are earned and players decide if a different amount of piggy banks could have been used.
5. Players take turns choosing dividends, deciding how many piggy banks, and distributing pennies.
6. The winner is the first player to score 50 points or greater.

Content Differentiation:

Moving Back: Use only the numbers that are multiples of 2, 5, or 10.

Moving Ahead: Play this game with the goal of having a remainder and/or use more piggy banks.

Piggy Banks

Piggy Banks

Piggy Banks

CONCEPT:
Rectangular Arrays for Multiplication and Division

 ## What are Rectangular Arrays for Multiplication and Division?

Beginning with single-digits, students can model multiplication and division with rectangular arrays. To construct a rectangular array, students form or draw equal rows. For example, 4 x 8 or 32 ÷ 8 is shown as:

Initially, students may count by ones to find the product/dividend. Building on this knowledge, we can encourage students to skip count and recognize the array without having to count all. After students gain comfort with single-digits, they can use rectangular arrays to solve multiplication and division problems with multi-digits.

 ## Formative Assessment

To find out if a student understands rectangular arrays for multiplication and division, ask the student to draw a rectangular array for the following expressions;

3 x 10
7 x 4

21 ÷ 7
40 ÷ 8

Notice how the student illustrates the arrays. Provide easier or more difficult expressions based on the student's degree of success with these problems.

Successful Strategies

Some teachers become too focused on rows versus columns when teaching rectangular arrays. By most definitions, rows are horizontal and columns are vertical. However, if you turn the array 90° the rows and columns switch. What complicates the issue further is that some educators use the term "rows" to mean both columns and rows. To deal with these complications, explain the inconsistencies to students and let them decide how they would like to use the terms in their descriptions of arrays. In this way, students can take ownership and focus on building meaningful experiences with multiplication and division.

> ### Math Words to Use
>
> **rectangular array,**
> **rows, columns, multiply,**
> **multiplication, multiplier,**
> **multiplicand, product**
> **divide, division, dividend,**
> **divisor, quotient**

  ## Questions at Different *Levels of Cognitive Demand*

EASY

Recall: *What are three rows of two?*

Comprehension: *What are rectangular arrays?*

Application: *How would you show the array for 9 x 4?*

Analysis: *Which array matches the expression?*

Evaluation: *What is the most important thing about rectangular arrays?*

Synthesis: *How would you recognize the array to show a different problem with the same product/dividend?*

COMPLEX

Frogs on a Log

A game designed to build the concept of rectangular arrays for multiplication and division

Materials:

- **100 small plastic frogs (or centimeter cubes to represent frogs)**
- **10 craft sticks (popsicle sticks)**
- **One 1-10 Spinner copied on white paper, paper clip**
- **One 1-10 Spinner copied on green paper, paper clip**
- **Dry erase boards and markers (or paper and pencil) for each player**

PLAYERS: 3 OR MORE

Directions:

1. **The first player spins the white spinner to determine the number of logs. The player displays this number with craft sticks lined up side-by-side.**
2. **The same player spins the green spinner to determine the number of frogs on each log. The player displays the frogs on the logs.**
3. **The other players illustrate the rectangular array using squares or circles on dry erase boards. The players also write the multiplication equation:** $\boxed{\text{white}}$ **X** $\boxed{\text{green}}$ **=** $\boxed{\text{product}}$
4. **The first player with the correct array and equation scores 100 points.**
5. **Players take turns modeling frogs on logs, drawing, and writing equations.**
6. **The winner is the first to score 1,000 or greater.**

Content Differentiation:

Moving Back: **Use white and green dice labeled 1-6 with numerals.**

Moving Ahead: **Play this game by writing division equations or both multiplication and division equations with or without the models.**

1-10 Spinner

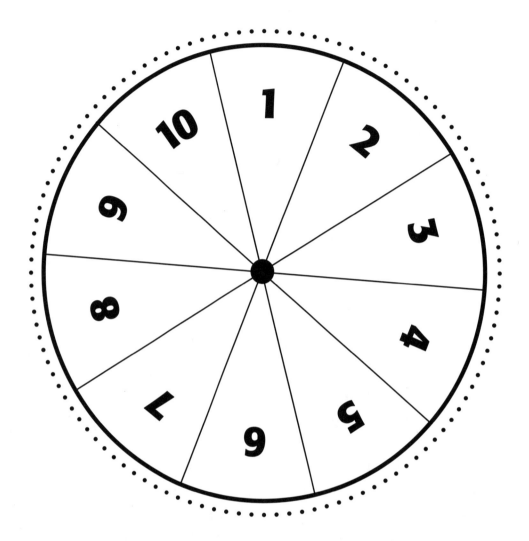

To use the spinner, place a paper clip in the center. Place pencil point through the paper clip at the center of the spinner. Holding the pencil securely with one hand, spin the paper clip with the other hand.

Multiplying and Dividing by Ten

What is the Multiplying and Dividing by Ten Concept?

Multiplying and dividing by ten builds fluency with number relationships and computation. When students understand the multiplying and dividing by ten concept, they are more apt to use mental math to solve problems and verify answers. Initially, students multiply ten by single-digit numbers and use 2-digit dividends to divide by ten. Building on this idea, they can learn to work with numbers having greater than 2-digits.

Formative Assessment

To find out if a student can multiply and divide by ten ask the student to solve the following equations;

2 x 10 =
4 x 10 =
5 x 10 =

$40 \div 10 =$
$60 \div 10 =$
$90 \div 10 =$

Ask the student to explain how he solved each problem. Analyze the student's level of proficiency through their accuracy, speed, and explanations.

Successful Strategies

One of the foundational concepts associated with multiplying and dividing by ten is rational counting by tens. Encourage students to skip count by tens starting with zero to help them learn the multiples of ten. To further help students understand the multiplying and dividing by ten concept, use base ten blocks or other manipulatives to model the operations.

> ## Math Words to Use
>
> **tens, multiply, multiplication, divide, division, times sign, division sign**

 Questions at Different *Levels of Cognitive Demand*

EASY

Recall: *What is 5 x 10?*

Comprehension: *How do you multiply a number by ten?*

Application: *How would you use 7 x 10 to solve 70 ÷ 10?*

Analysis: *Which facts are not directly related to multiples of ten?*

Evaluation: *How would you recommend that someone learn how to multiply and divide by ten?*

Synthesis: *How could you use the multiplying and dividing by ten concept to multiply and divide by nine?*

COMPLEX

Turtle Race

A game designed to build the concept of multiplying and dividing by ten

PLAYERS: 2

Materials:

- Decahedron die (labeled 0-9) or 0-9 spinner
- Turtle Race Game Board (Multiplication)
- 2 small plastic turtles (or cubes to represent turtles)

Directions:

1. Each player places a turtle on one of the start boxes.
2. The first player rolls the die (or spins spinner). The number showing is multiplied by ten. The player can move her turtle if the product is in a box that is touching the box that the turtle is currently occupying. Moves can be forward, backward, vertical, horizontal, or diagonal. If the player cannot move, she misses her turn. If a move is possible, the player must move her turtle (even backwards).
3. The next player rolls the die (or spins the spinner) and moves his turtle, if possible. Both turtles can occupy the same box at the same time, if necessary.
4. Players take turns. The winner is the first turtle to reach the finish line.

Content Differentiation:

Moving Back: Use a hundred chart as a reference. Model equations with base ten blocks.

Moving Ahead: Play the divide by ten version of this game by using numeral cards (0, 10, 20, 30, 40, 50, 60, 70, 80, 90) instead of die or spinner with the Turtle Race (Division) game board. Or add zero to each value on the multiplication game board and multiply by 100.

0-9 Spinner

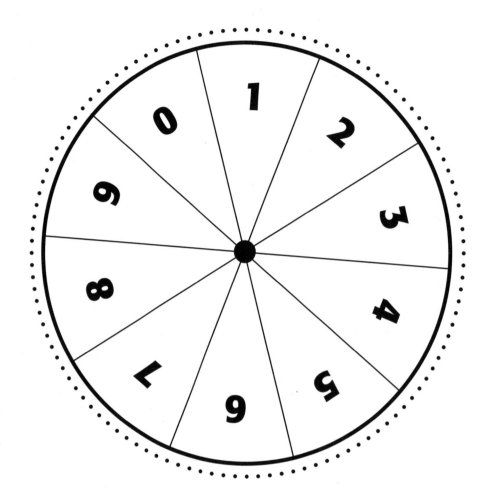

To use the spinner, place a paper clip in the center. Place pencil point through the paper clip at the center of the spinner. Holding the pencil securely with one hand, spin the paper clip with the other hand.

Turtle Race Game Board
(Multiplication)

0	Start	30	0	70	40	10	Start	40
10	70	40	10	80	50	20	80	50
20	80	50	20	90	60	30	90	60
30	90	60	30	0	70	40	0	70
40	0	70	40	10	80	50	10	80
50	10	80	50	20	90	60	20	90
60	20	90	60 Finish Line	30 Finish Line	0 Finish Line	70	30	0

Turtle Race Game Board
(Division)

0	Start	3	0	7	4	1	Start	4
1	7	4	1	8	5	2	8	5
2	8	5	2	9	6	3	9	6
3	9	6	3	0	7	4	0	7
4	0	7	4	1	8	5	1	8
5	1	8	5	2	9	6	2	9
6	2	9	6 Finish Line	3 Finish Line	0 Finish Line	7	3	0

Math Intervention: Grades 3-5 • *Jennifer Taylor-Cox* • © *Eye On Education*

Perfect Squares and Near Squares

What is the Perfect Squares and Near Squares Concept?

As with adding doubles, there is something uniquely fascinating about multiplying a number with itself. Often students' levels of interest are elevated, which prompts them to master perfect squares earlier than other multiplication facts. The smaller squares (1 x 1, 2 x 2, 3 x 3, 4 x 4, 5 x 5) and interesting squares (such as 10 x 10) are commonly learned quickly. Sometimes the larger squares (6 x 6, 7 x 7, 8 x 8, 9 x 9, 11 x 11, 12 x 12) take more time. Students require many experiences with perfect squares. When students own these facts, they are ready to use this knowledge to solve near squares multiplication problems. When teaching the near squares concept, encourage students to identify the two perfect squares that the near square falls between and encourage them to use plus or minus one group to solve the equation. For example, the near square 8 x 7 = 56 falls between 7 x 7 = 49 and 8 x 8 = 64. If a student uses 7 x 7, he will add one more group of seven (49 + 7 = 56). If he uses 8 x 8, he will subtract one group of eight (64 – 8 = 56). Rather than providing rules for students to follow, allow students to decide which perfect square fact they want to use to solve the near square problem so that they understand the math more completely.

Formative Assessment

To find out if a student understands perfect squares and near squares ask the student to solve several squares (3 x 3, 5 x 5, 7 x 7, 9 x 9) and near squares (2 x 3, 5 x 4, 6 x 7, 7 x 8) multiplication problems. Notice how quickly the student solves the problems. Ask students to explain how they solved the problems to find out if they are using perfect squares and near squares.

Successful Strategies

Teaching students to identify perfect squares and near squares is the first step in ownership of these facts. Ask students to explain which two squares "sandwich" the near square. Use manipulatives and graph paper arrays to model one more group and one less group. Write the facts in order so students can see the patterns. As students gain ownership of perfect squares and near squares, we need to encourage them to use this knowledge with related division facts.

> ## Math Words to Use
>
> **perfect squares, near squares, product, multiply, multiplication, groups, sets, multiplier, multiplicand, facts**

 ## Questions at Different *Levels of Cognitive Demand*

EASY

Recall: *What is 5 x 5?*

Comprehension: *What example could you give of a perfect square multiplication fact?*

Application: *How would you show near squares products with graph paper arrays?*

Analysis: *Which factor of the near square fact do you plan to use?*

Evaluation: *How would you teach near squares to someone who does not understand it?*

Synthesis: *How could you create a perfect squares and near squares game?*

COMPLEX

X Marks the Spot (Multiplication)

*A game designed to build the concept
of perfect squares and near squares*

**PLAYERS:
2**

Materials:

- **Decahedron die (labeled 0-9) or
  0-9 spinner** *(see page 102)*
- **X Marks the Spot Game Board for
  Perfect Squares Products**
- **Two highlighters or light markers (different colors)**

Directions:

1. Players decide which color highlighter each person will use.
2. The first player rolls the die or spins the spinner. The player
   multiplies the number with itself and looks for the perfect
   square product on the game board.
3. The player marks the product with a dot using the highlighter
   to "hold" the spot.
4. The next player rolls or spins a number, multiplies the
   number with itself and looks for the perfect square product
   on the game board. The player can mark the product with
   a dot to hold it OR the player can "claim" any product that
   is currently being held with a dot. If the player claims a held
   product, she uses the highlighter to draw X on the product.
5. Players take turns choosing numbers, multiplying, and
   holding or claiming products. *NOTE: All products must be
   held before they are claimed and can be claimed by* <u>*any*</u> *player.*
6. The winner is the first player to have four claimed products
   (Xs) in a row (horizontal, vertical, or diagonal).

Content Differentiation:

Moving Back: **Play the game without holding prior to claiming.**

Moving Ahead: **Play the same game using Near Squares
Products instead of Square Products. The near square is one
more group or one less group than a perfect square.**

X Marks the Spot Game Board
for Perfect Squares Products

X Marks the Spot Game Board
for Near Squares Products

CONCEPT:
Near Tens for Multiplication

 ## What is the Near Tens for Multiplication Concept?

The near tens concept involves adjusting multiplication facts based on their proximity to tens facts. The near tens concept can be used with the nines facts, for example, 9 x 7 = (10 x 7) – (1 x 7). If can also be used with eights facts, for example, 8 x 7 = (10 x 7) – (2 x 7). Additionally, the near tens concept can be used with the elevens facts, for example, 11 x 7 = (10 x 7) + (1 x 7) and the twelves facts, for example, 12 x 7 = (10 x 7) + (2 x 7). While the same type of adjustments can be applied to any facts, the near tens concept is most applicable to the 9s, 8s, 11s, and 12s multiplication facts. When students use the near tens concept, they apply the kind of flexibility with numbers which is needed for mental math and deep conceptual understanding.

 ## Formative Assessment

To find out if a student understands the near tens for multiplication concept, ask the student to solve the following equations;

6 x 10 =	10 x 8 =
7 x 9 =	9 x 5 =
4 x 8 =	8 x 6 =
11 x 7 =	9 x 11 =
5 x 12 =	8 x 12 =

Have the student explain how he solves each problem. If the student uses the traditional algorithm (successfully or not successfully), ask the student if he knows another way to solve the equations. Invite the student to try the problems using what they know about multiplying tens.

Successful Strategies

To be successful with the near tens multiplication concept, students must have ownership of multiplying and dividing ten. The near tens concept builds upon what students know about multiplying and dividing tens. For many students, using a multiplication chart helps them to see and apply the near tens concept.

Math Words to Use
near ten, multiply, multiplication, divide, division, adjust, compensate

Questions at Different *Levels of Cognitive Demand*

EASY

Recall: *What is 9 x 10?*

Comprehension: *How could you use a near ten to solve 9 x 6?*

Application: *How would you show the near tens concept with manipulatives?*

Analysis: *Which problems invite the near tens concept?*

Evaluation: *When is it ineffective to use the near tens concept?*

Synthesis: *How would you teach the near tens concept to someone who did not know it?*

COMPLEX

Roll and Flip

A game designed to build the concept of near tens for multiplication and division

Materials:

PLAYERS: 2 OR MORE

- **Die with six sides labeled 10 x, 10 x, 9 x, 9 x, 8 x, 8 x**
- **0-9 Number Cards** *(see page 50)*

Directions:

1. **Players shuffle and distribute cards face down.**
2. **The first player rolls the die and flips one of her cards. If the player rolls 10 x, she multiplies ten times the number on the card. If the player rolls 9 x or 8 x, she uses the 10 times multiplication fact to mentally solve it. For example, 4 x 9 = (4 x 10) – (4 x 1).**
3. **The player must describe how she uses the near tens concept. The product is the player's score for that round.**
4. **Players take turns rolling the die, flipping cards, and using near tens to solve the problems.**
5. **Play continues for ten rounds. Players add their scores from each round. The winner is the player with the highest score.**

Content Differentiation:

Moving Back: Use a die with only 10 x and 9 x.

Moving Ahead: Include the related division equations for each round. Change the die to include 11 x and 12 x.

Fact Families—Multiplication and Division

 What are Fact Families for Multiplication and Division?

Fact families for multiplication and division are facts that are directly related. In the fact family, there are two multiplication problems and two division problems. The multiplication facts are manifestations of the commutative property because changing the order does not change the result of the operation. The division facts are inverse operations of the multiplication facts.

 Formative Assessment

To find out if a student understands multiplication and division fact families, provide the following incomplete fact family and ask the student which fact is missing from the family;

7 x 5 = 35
35 ÷ 7 = 5
35 ÷ 5 = 7

If the student is not successful, try fact families with smaller numbers. If the student is successful, ask him to generate all of the facts in the 6, 9, 54 fact family.

Successful Strategies

Some students struggle with fact families. One of the ways to help these students is to go back to the repeated addition and repeated subtraction concepts. Focusing on the "groups" encourages students to think about the related multiplication and division facts. Additionally, help student to see why squares produce identical facts.

Math Words to Use

multiplication, division, equation, facts, fact families, groups

Questions at Different *Levels of Cognitive Demand*

EASY

Recall: *What is 5 x 4? What is 4 x 5?*

Comprehension: *How would you explain fact families?*

Application: *How would you show the fact family for 6, 8, 48?*

Analysis: *What relationship do you see between 7 x 6 and 42 ÷ 6?*

Evaluation: *What advice would you give someone who does not understand fact families?*

Synthesis: *Is it possible to have a fact family for this equation 2 x 3 x 4 = 24?*

COMPLEX

Fishy Facts

A game designed to build the concept of multiplication and division fact families

Materials:

- Fishy Facts resource pages, scissors
- Bowl

PLAYERS: 3 OR MORE

Directions:

1. Cut out fish and place in a bowl.
2. One player reaches into the bowl and pulls out one fish. The player displays the fish to other players.
3. When displaying a fish, the player holds the fish by the tail or one of the fins to cover up one of the numbers in the fact family.
4. The first player to correctly identify the covered number has an opportunity to earn the fish by naming all four facts in the fact family.
5. Players take turns displaying fish, identifying covered numbers, and naming facts in fact families.
6. The winner is the player with the most fish after all (or a specified number) of the fish are displayed.

Content Differentiation:

Moving Back: Use selected fish (2s, 5s, 10s).

Moving Ahead: Use the blank fish to make different fact families.

Fishy Facts

Fishy Facts

Partial Products

 ## What is the Partial Products Concept?

The partial products concept is a multiplication strategy that involves breaking down a larger problem into smaller, more manageable problems. The traditional algorithm for multiplication involves procedures, such as *aligning digits in columns* and *always starting with the ones*. For many students the rules of the traditional algorithm are meaningless. They cannot remember what to do because they do not understand the math. Alternatives to algorithms such as partial products help build students' conceptual understanding. With partial products, it does not matter if the columns are aligned or if the student starts with the ones or not. There is no need to "bring down a zero" or "put the big number on top." Let's look at 6 x 14. Using the distributive property, we break it down into smaller problems, 6 (10 + 4) = (6 x 10) + (6 x 4). In this situation, 60 is part of the product and 24 is part of the product. These partial products are easily combined into the total product of 84. Working with partial products builds students' conceptual understanding.

 ## Formative Assessment

To find out if a student understands the partial products concept ask the student to solve the following equations;

13 x 4 =	26 x 5 =	52 x 7 =
16 x 12 =	18 x 27 =	46 x 27 =

Have the student explain how he solves each problem. If the student uses the traditional algorithm (successfully or not successfully), ask the student if he knows another way to solve the equations. Invite the student to try the problems without aligning the digits in columns and without starting with the ones.

Successful Strategies

One of the reasons students struggle with the traditional algorithm is due to the inaccurate descriptions of the procedures they have heard. Unfortunately, many people use digit names rather than number values, which create potential misconceptions for students. When solving 21 x 6, they may say 6 x 1 and 6 x 2. The accurate description is 6 x 1 and 6 x 20. The partial products concept is embedded in place value and conceptual understanding, which help remedy algorithmic misconceptions. Even if students successfully use the traditional algorithm, learning the partial products concept invites students to strengthen conceptual understanding, increase mental math capacity, and improve flexibility and fluency.

> ### Math Words to Use
>
> **partial, part, product, multiplication, multiply, equation, equal, distributive property**

 ## Questions at Different *Levels of Cognitive Demand*

EASY

Recall: *What is 27 x 8?*

Comprehension: *How did you solve the problem?*

Application: *What picture could you draw to show the partial products?*

Analysis: *How would you compare the partial products?*

Evaluation: *Which products are easier to work with? Why?*

Synthesis: *How would you design a template for recording partial products?*

COMPLEX

Products in Parts

*A game designed to build the concept
of partial products*

**PLAYERS:
3 OR MORE**

Materials:

- Several sheets of centimeter graph paper
- Highlighter for each player
- Base ten blocks
- Two red dice (labeled 1-6 with numerals)
- Two white dice (labeled 1-6 with numerals)
- Dry erase boards and markers (or paper and pencils)

Directions:

1. The first player rolls all four dice to generate a 2-digit times 2-digit multiplication equation. The red dice represent the tens and the white dice represent the ones.

2. The player shows the equation with lines and dots using the highlighter on graph paper. For example, 12 x 21 includes one line of ten and two dots of one *times* two lines of ten and one dot of one.

3. The player shows a model of the partial products by placing base ten blocks to show the array.

4. Other players race to record the partial products (10 x 20) + (10 x 1) + (2 x 20) + (2 x 1) = 200 + 10 + 40 + 2. The first player with the correct partial products scores 1,000 points.

5. Players take turns rolling, modeling and recording partial products. The winner is the first player to score 10,000.

Content Differentiation:

Moving Back: Try single-digit times 2-digit equations.

Moving Ahead: Use decahedron dice or 0-9 spinners.

CONCEPT:
Partial Quotients

 What is the Partial Quotients Concept?

The partial quotients concept is a division strategy that involves consecutive approximations. Like partial products, this concept serves as an alternative to the traditional algorithm. For some students the rules of long division are difficult to remember and they miss steps resulting in incorrect answers. The beauty of the partial quotients concept is the focus it has on building conceptual knowledge of division through estimation. Students estimate how many multiples of the divisor they should work with each time they divide. These partial quotients are combined to name the complete quotient. Remainders are easily identified.

$$14\overline{)1092}$$

```
14)1092
   - 700      50
   ─────
     392
   - 280      20
   ─────
     112
    - 70       5
   ─────
      42
    - 42       3
   ─────
       0
     R 0     78 Quotient
```

 Formative Assessment

To find out if a student understands partial quotients ask the student to solve the following equations;

$$5\overline{)125} \qquad 7\overline{)3360} \qquad 16\overline{)304} \qquad 42\overline{)7336}$$

Ask the student to explain how she solves each problem. If the she uses the traditional algorithm (successfully or not successfully), ask if she knows another way to solve the equations. Encourage the student to try using estimation to find parts of the quotient.

Successful Strategies

Encourage students to come up with ways to record the partial quotients. Students may decide to record the partial quotients with a different color marker, on a separate sheet of paper, or on sticky notes. If students figure out what works best for them, they are more likely to know what to do because they understand why it works. As with partial products, even if students successfully use the traditional algorithm, learning the partial quotients concept invites students to strengthen conceptual understanding, increase mental math capacity, and improve flexibility and fluency.

> **Math Words to Use**
>
> **partial, part, quotient, divide, division, strategy, equation, equal, dividend, divisor**

 ## Questions at Different *Levels of Cognitive Demand*

EASY

Recall: *What is 120 divided by five?*

Comprehension: *How would you divide 270 by 45?*

Application: *How do you show a remainder?*

Analysis: *How would you categorize your partial quotients?*

Evaluation: *Which initial partial quotient do you recommend? Why?*

Synthesis: *What if the remainder was divided into fractions?*

COMPLEX

Prove It

A game designed to build the concept of partial quotients

Materials:

PLAYERS: 2 OR MORE TEAMS

- Three blue dice (labeled 1-6)
- Two yellow dice (labeled 1-6)
- Dry erase boards and marker (or paper and pencil) for each team
- 2-minute timer

Directions:

1. The first team rolls all three blue dice. The team arranges the dice in any way to show the 3-digit number that will serve as the dividend.
2. The other team rolls both yellow dice. The team arranges the dice in any way to show the 2-digit number that will serve as the divisor.
3. The timer is set. All teams write the division problem on dry erase boards and work together to solve the equation using partial quotients.
4. Any team that correctly solves the equation using partial quotients in under two minutes earns points for the round. The quotient tells how many points are earned for the round.
5. Before erasing boards for the next round, players must prove their use of partial quotients, compare answers, and discuss which partial quotients were used and why.
6. Teams keep a running total of points earned. After ten rounds, the team with the most points wins.

Content Differentiation:

Moving Back: Use two blue dice and one yellow die.

Moving Ahead: Use four blue dice and three yellow dice.

Equal Products

 ## What is the Equal Products Concept?

The equal products concept is a multiplication strategy based on the idea that different multiplication equations can have the same product. This concept involves manipulating the multiplicand and the multiplier in a way that results in the same product. We can double the multiplicand and halve the multiplier (or vice versa) to create a new expression that has the same product, for example, 25 x 6 = 50 x 3. In this and other situations, doubling and halving to produce equal products results in a problem that is easier to mentally solve. The key is to know when this concept is most applicable. Using the equal products concept helps students understand number relationships and builds conceptual knowledge of multiplication and division.

 ## Formative Assessment

To find out if a student understands the equal products concept, ask the student to solve the following equations;

15 x 2 =   25 x 12 =   35 x 6 =   75 x 16 =

Ask the student explain how he solves each problem. If the student uses the traditional algorithm (successfully or not successfully), ask him if he knows another way to solve the equations. Encourage the students to solve the problems using what they know about doubling and halving.

Successful Strategies

While the equal products concept can be used in any multiplication situation, it is most efficient when the newly created expression invites mental math. We need to teach students to get a feel for the numbers they are working with. Is the multiplicand (or multiplier) a number that is easier to work with when it is doubled? Is the multiplier (or multiplicand) even? Students must learn how to analyze multiplication equations to help them figure out which concept is preferred. For some students the equal products concept is a mystery. If they do not understand why the doubling and halving procedures work, they will not build conceptual understanding of multiplication. One of the best ways to model the equal products concept is with arrays. If we have a paper array that is 25 x 6, we can cut the array and slide part of it to show 50 x 3.

> ## Math Words to Use
>
> **product, multiplicand, multiplier, multiplication, multiply, equal, equation, expression**

 Questions at Different *Levels of Cognitive Demand*

EASY

Recall: *What is 25 x 8?*

Comprehension: *How would you solve 35 x 6?*

Application: *Where would you cut and how would you move the array to show an equal product?*

Analysis: *How would you compare and contrast the products?*

Evaluation: *Is equal products always the most efficient way to solve an equation? Why?*

COMPLEX

Synthesis: *What if we quadrupled the multiplier?*

That's It

A game designed to build the concept
of equal products

Materials:

- 15-95 Spinner copied on yellow paper, paper clip
- 2-18 Spinner copied on pink paper, paper clip
- Timer and calculator

PLAYERS: 2 OR MORE

Directions:

1. The first player spins the yellow spinner to find the multiplicand and spins the pink spinner to find the multiplier.

2. The player states the multiplication equation while the other player starts the timer. The player doubles the multiplicand, halves the multiplier, and states the equal products. For example the player says, "45 x 4 = 90 x 2. *That's it!* 180."

3. The other player stops the timer. The number of seconds is recorded as the player's score. Players keep a running total throughout the game.

4. After each player has one turn the round is complete. After each round, the spinners alternate. The pink spinner is the multiplicand and the yellow spinner is the multiplier.

5. Players take turns spinning, creating and stating equal products, timing each other, and verifying answers with the calculator.

6. The winner is the player with the lowest score after ten rounds.

Content Differentiation:

Moving Back: Using a graph paper array for each equation, cut and move the array to model the doubling and halving.

Moving Ahead: Make a new pink spinner with larger even numbers.

15-95 Spinner

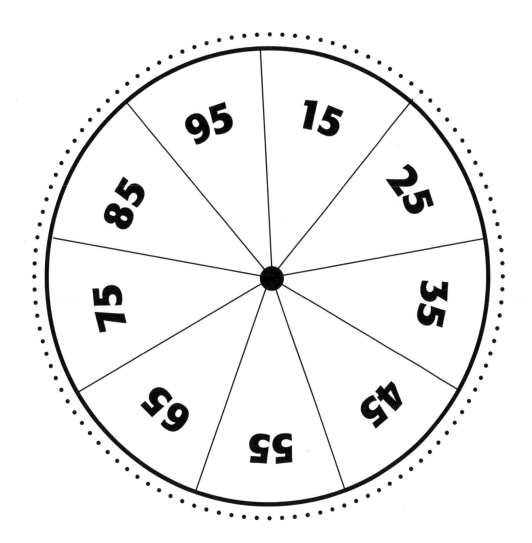

To use the spinner, place a paper clip in the center. Place pencil point through the paper clip at the center of the spinner. Holding the pencil securely with one hand, spin the paper clip with the other hand.

2-18 Spinner

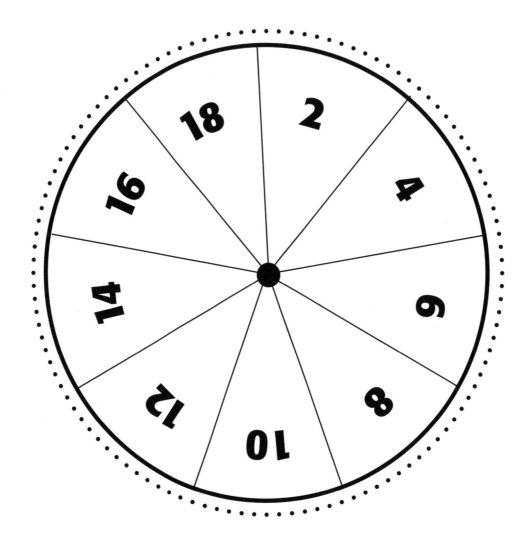

To use the spinner, place a paper clip in the center. Place pencil point through the paper clip at the center of the spinner. Holding the pencil securely with one hand, spin the paper clip with the other hand.

CHAPTER

Multifaceted Number Concepts

Expanded Form

Thousands and Millions

Commutative and Associative Properties

Prime and Composite Numbers

Finding Common Multiples

Finding Common Factors

Adding and Subtracting Fractions

Rename Fractions as Decimals

Compare and Order Fractions
and Mixed Numbers

CONCEPT:
Expanded Form

 What is the Expanded Form Concept?

Expanded form involves expressing a number as a sum of the products of each digit. The expanded form concept is deeply rooted in place value. Expressing the value of any number by highlighting the parts of that number helps students build fluency with numbers. Working with expanded form also helps students understand how numbers are composed and decomposed.

 Formative Assessment

To find out if a student understands expanded form, ask the student to name the values for the following expanded form expressions;

(4 x 10) + (8 x 1)   (3 x 100) + (5 x 10) + (3 x 1)

(7 x 100) + (6 x 1)   (2 x 1,000) + (3 x 100) + (9 x 10) + (1 x 1)

(7 x 1,000) + (8 x 100) + (3 x 1)   (4 x 10,000) + (6 x 100) + (5 x 10)

Ask the student to give the expanded form of the following numbers;

63   425

907   4,820

6,039   24,309

Find out the range of the student's knowledge of the expanded form concept by identifying to which place value the student is successful.

Successful Strategies

To help strengthen understanding of the expanded form concept students need to build numbers with place value manipulatives (such as base ten blocks and Digi-Blocks™). As students build numbers, they need to discuss what the values look like and the differences among values within the number. The math discourse combined with the visualization and manipulation is powerful for students.

Math Words to Use

expanded form, digits,
values, expression, equation

Questions at Different *Levels of Cognitive Demand*

EASY

Recall: *What is (5 x 100) + (3 x 10) + (7 x 1)?*

Comprehension: *What is expanded form?*

Application: *How would you show 3,268 in expanded form?*

Analysis: *How would you compare the parts of expanded form?*

Evaluation: *Why is expanded form a helpful way to show numbers?*

Synthesis: *How would you use expanded form with decimal fractions?*

COMPLEX

Race Track

A game designed to build the concept of expanded form

PLAYERS: 2 OR MORE

Materials:

- 4 dice (labeled 1-6 with numerals) for each player
- Race Track for each player
- Pencil or pen for each player

Directions:

1. Players say, "On your mark. Get set. Go!"
2. Players roll all four dice and form a 4-digit number with the numbers rolled.
3. Players write this number on the first speed limit sign and write the expanded form of this number in the first section of the race track.
4. As soon as the section of the race track is complete, the player rolls again and repeats the process.
5. All players are filling in individual race tracks at the same time.
6. The winner is the first player to accurately complete his race track.
7. Answers are verified by other players after the game.

Content Differentiation:

Moving Back: Use three dice for 3-digit numbers.

Moving Ahead: Use more than four dice for larger numbers.

Race Track

Thousands and Millions

What is the Thousands and Millions Concept?

Using a positional system, digits occupy places to name number values. Some students struggle with multi-digit numbers. Students end up reading digits rather than reading the actual number because these large numbers do not have meaning to the students.

Millions			Thousands			Ones		
hundreds	tens	ones	hundreds	tens	ones	hundreds	tens	ones
1	3	5	7	9	2	4	6	8

The number is *one hundred, thirty-five million, seven hundred ninety-two thousand, four hundred sixty-eight*. Provide students with meaningful experiences which include seeing, hearing, and building numbers.

Formative Assessment

To find out if a student understands thousands and millions ask the student to write the following numbers with digits;

One thousand, eight hundred, forty-nine
Two hundred thousand, seven hundred, eight
Five million, six thousand, two hundred, fifty-three

Ask the student to read the following numbers;

4,357   93,618   6,278,021   23,062,340

Successful Strategies

To help students gain comfort with large numbers we can provide them with representations. Ask students to examine 10,000 dots *(see page 136)* to build meaning for the value. By making 100 copies of the 10,000 dots, we can provide a representation of 1,000,000 for students. Additionally, model math language as numbers are read with students.

Math Words to Use

ones, tens, hundreds, thousands, ten thousand, hundred thousand, million, ten million, hundred million

Questions at Different *Levels of Cognitive Demand*

EASY

Recall: *Which place is between thousands and tens?*

Comprehension: *How many zeros are in ten thousand?*

Application: *How would you show 20,000?*

Analysis: *How would you compare 10,000 to 100,000?*

Evaluation: *What do you recommend for someone who does not understand millions?*

Synthesis: *How would you design a place value chart that includes decimals?*

COMPLEX

Ten Thousand Dots

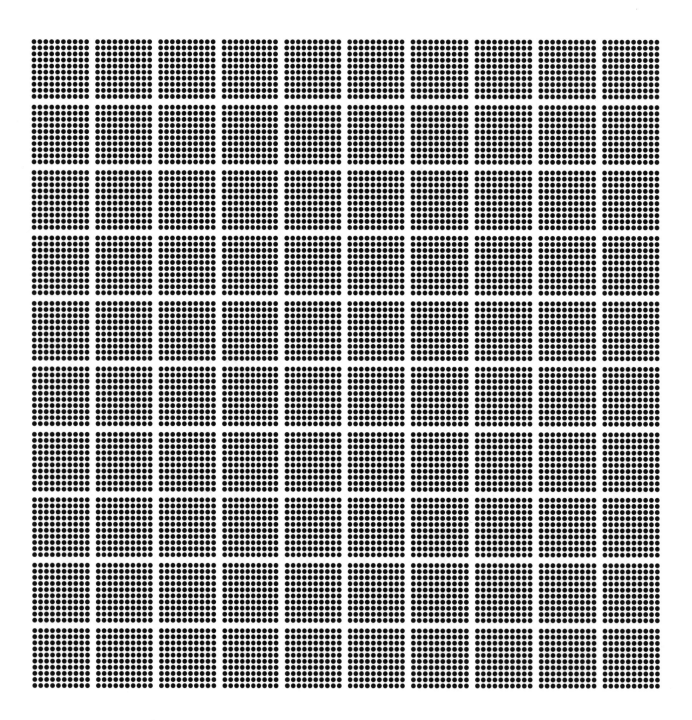

Which Place is Best?

*A game designed to build the concept
of thousands and millions*

**PLAYERS:
2 OR MORE**

Materials:

- **Place Value Frame for each player**
- **Die (labeled 1-6 or 0-9)**
- **Pencil or pen for each player**
- **File folder for each player**

Directions:

1. **The first player rolls the die. All players write this number in any one of the spaces on their place value frames. Players use the file folders to keep the other players from seeing where they placed the digit. Once a number is placed, it cannot be moved.**

2. **Players take turns rolling the die and placing digits in either the first number or the second number until all of the sections are filled.**

3. **Players lift the file folders to reveal their numbers. Players read and compare the numbers. The player with the largest first number earns 1,000,000 points. The player with the largest second number earns 1,000,000 points.**

4. **Play continues with players accumulating points until the winning player earns 10,000,000 points!**

Content Differentiation:

Moving Back: **Use fewer sections in the place value frames.**

Moving Ahead: **Include a decimal point somewhere on each place value frame.**

*NOTE: This game appears in Taylor-Cox, J. (2005) **Family Math Night: Math Standards in Action**. Eye on Education.*

Place Value Frames

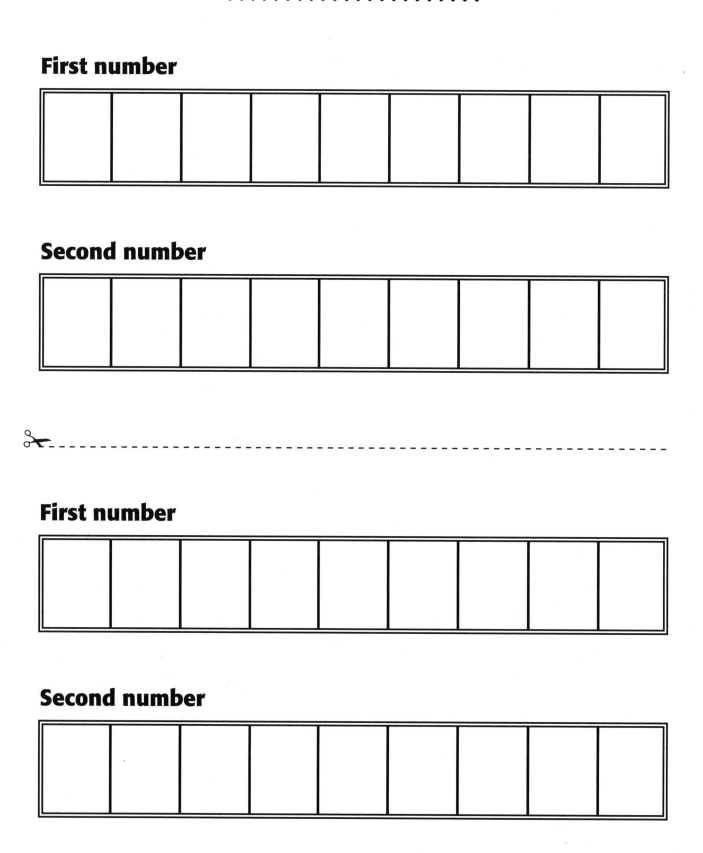

First number

Second number

First number

Second number

Commutative and Associative Properties

 What are the Commutative and Associative Properties?

What are the commutative and associative properties? The commutative property involves changing the order of the operations of numbers without changing the result. Students work with foundational ideas of the commutative property, also called the order property, when they work with fact families. They learn that $3 + 5 = 5 + 3$ and $6 \times 8 = 8 \times 6$. It is important for students to understand that addition and multiplication have the commutative property, while subtraction and division do not. Similarly, the associative property involves changing the grouping of the numbers without changing the result. $(2 + 7) + 3 = 2 + (7 + 3)$ and $(4 \times 5) \times 2 = 4 \times (5 \times 2)$. Students must understand that addition and multiplication have the associative property, while subtraction and division do not.

 Formative Assessment

To find out if a student understands the commutative and associative properties ask the students to identify which property (commutative or associative), if any, the following equations represent;

$8 + 7 = 7 + 8$

$2 + (5 + 3) = (2 + 5) + 3$

$(5 \times 2) \times 3 = 5 \times (2 \times 3)$

$3 \times 7 = 7 \times 3$

$(6 + 8) + 9 = (8 + 6) + 9$

Successful Strategies

Analyzing equations to find out if the order is changed or the groupings are changed is an important aspect of understanding the commutative and associate properties. It is critical that students also experience situations that involve addition and multiplication so that they learn when the properties may not be applicable.

> ## Math Words to Use
>
> **commutative property, order, associative property, grouping, addition, multiplication, sum, product, expression, equation**

 ## Questions at Different *Levels of Cognitive Demand*

EASY

Recall: *Does 5 + 3 = 3 + 4?*

Comprehension: *Why does 6 x 7 = 7 x 6?*

Application: *How would you show the commutative property using the digits 3, 4, 5?*

Analysis: *How would you compare the associative and commutative properties?*

Evaluation: *What is the value in knowing the commutative and associative properties?*

Synthesis: *How would you rearrange an expression that includes addition and multiplication to make a different, yet equal expression?*

COMPLEX

Baseball

A game designed to build the concepts of commutative and associative properties

Materials:

PLAYERS: 2 OR MORE

- Baseball Spinner, paper clip
- 3 dice (labeled 1-6 with numerals)
- Baseball Field resource page
- Pawns of a different color for each player
- Dry erase board and marker for each player

Directions:

1. To begin the first round, a player spins the spinner. If it lands on single or double, the player rolls two dice. If it lands on triple or homerun, the player rolls three dice.
2. All players use the numbers rolled to write the type of equation shown on the spinner on their dry erase boards.
3. The first player to write the correct equation and call out the correct sum or product moves her pawn on the baseball field. For example, $(3 + 2) + 4 = 3 + (2 + 4)$ has a sum of nine. The player moves her pawn to third base.
4. Players take turns spinning the spinner and rolling the dice for each new round. Players can occupy the same base at the same time.
5. If a player's pawn is on second base and the player scores a single, she moves the pawn to third base. However, players can not score more than one run per round. For example, if a player's pawn is on third base and the player scores a double, she can only go to home plate.
6. Play continues until a player score five runs.

Content Differentiation:

Moving Back: Play this game using only the commutative property (singles and doubles).

Moving Ahead: Use parentheses in all equations.

Baseball Spinner

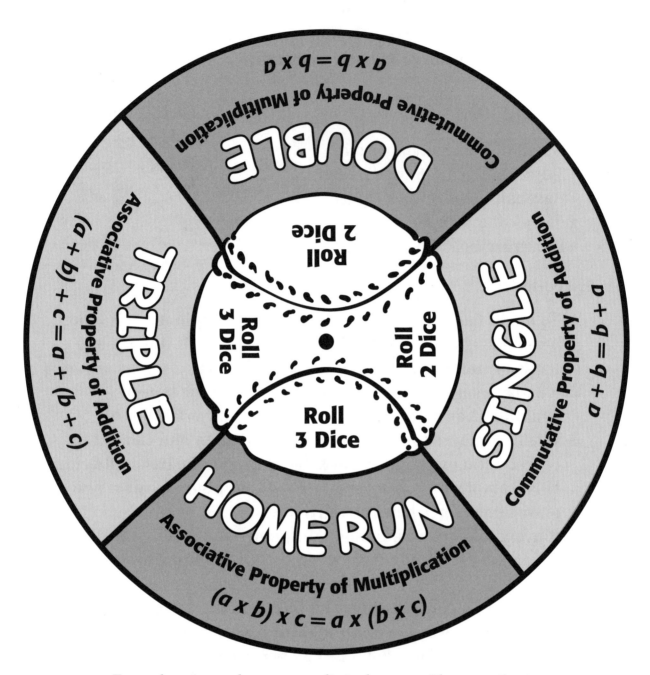

To use the spinner, place a paper clip in the center. Place pencil point through the paper clip at the center of the spinner. Holding the pencil securely with one hand, spin the paper clip with the other hand.

Baseball Field

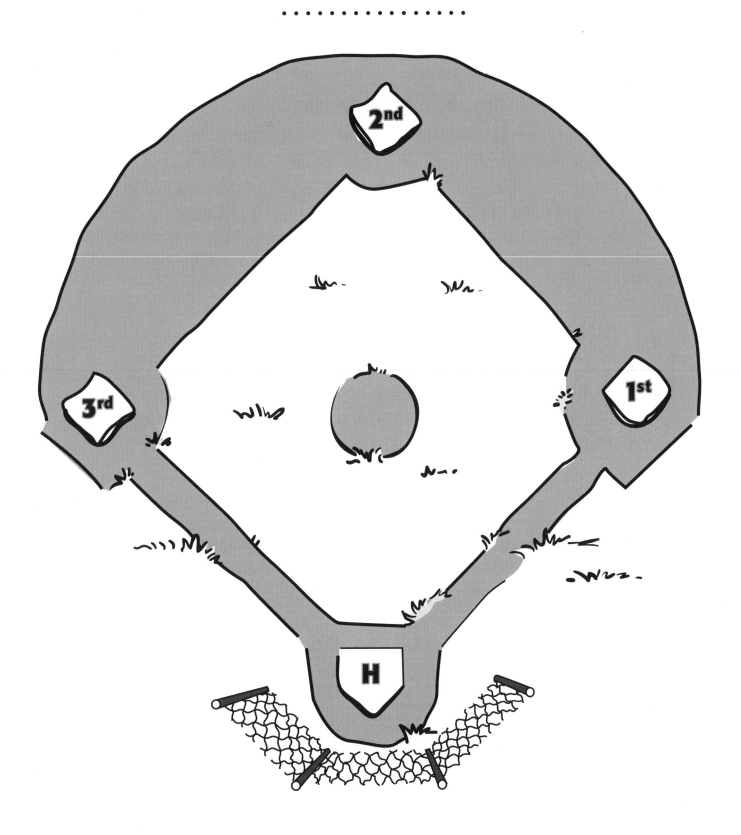

Prime and Composite Numbers

What are Prime and Composite Numbers?

Prime numbers have exactly two factors. These factors are 1 and the number itself. For example, 2 is a prime number because its only factors are 1 and 2. Composite numbers have more than two factors. For example, 12 is a composite number because it is divisible by 1, 2, 3, 4, 6, and 12. One is not considered a prime number or a composite number. Prime factorization involves renaming a composite number as a product of prime numbers.

Formative Assessment

To find out if a student understands prime and composite numbers ask the students to use factor trees to show the prime factorization of the following numbers;

12   24   32   100

If the students are unfamiliar with factor trees, display the factor tree for 12 and ask them to explain the relationships they see within the factor tree as a springboard for making their own factor trees.

Successful Strategies

Prime factorization helps students identify and understand prime and composite numbers because students are able to see how numbers are decomposed using multiplication and division. When making a factor tree, encourage students to continue finding factors until all the factors are prime numbers. When students are ready, encourage them to record the prime factorization with exponents.

Math Words to Use

prime number, composite number, factor, factorization, factor tree, divisible

  ## Questions at Different *Levels of Cognitive Demand*

EASY

Recall: *Is 5 a prime number?*

Comprehension: *Why is 10 a composite number?*

Application: *How would you show the prime factorization of 8?*

Analysis: *How would you compare the prime and composite numbers?*

Evaluation: *What is the value in knowing how to make a factor tree?*

Synthesis: *What if we needed to show prime factorization without a factor tree?*

COMPLEX

Prime Time

A game designed to build the concepts of prime and composite numbers

Materials:

PLAYERS: 2 OR MORE

- Dry erase board and marker for each player
- 0-9 Number Cards copied on yellow paper *(see page 50)*
- 0-9 Number Cards copied on green paper *(see page 50)*

Directions:

1. Players shuffle each set of number cards and place them face down in two piles.
2. To begin the first round, a player chooses one yellow number card and one green number card to make a 2-digit number. The yellow card serves as the tens digit and the green card serves as the ones digit. *NOTE: If a yellow zero is drawn, the number will be a single digit number.*
3. If the number formed with the cards is a prime number, the player earns five points and the turn is complete. If the number formed is a composite number, the players race to draw factor trees for the number on dry erase boards. The first player to complete the factor tree calls out "Prime Factorization Complete!" If her factor tree is accurate, she earns ten points. If the factor tree is not accurate, she earns zero points.
4. Players continue taking turns choosing cards, identifying prime numbers, drawing factor trees, and keeping a running total.
5. The first player to reach a score of 50 calls out "Prime Time" and is the winner. *NOTE: Number cards can be shuffled and reused.*

Content Differentiation:

Moving Back: Play this game using dice (labeled 1-6) instead of 0-9 number cards.

Moving Ahead: Players write equations with exponents after they draw the factor trees.

CONCEPT:
Finding Common Multiples

 What is the Finding Common Multiples Concept?

Multiples of a number are the product of multiplying that number by another whole number. For example, 18 is a multiple of 3 because 3 x 6 = 18. Three has other multiples, too; 3, 6, 9, 12, 15, 21, 24, 27, 30, ... Often the task is to find common multiples of two or more numbers. For example, 24 is a common multiple of 6 and 8 because 24 is a multiple of 6 and of 8. Every multiple of 24 is also a multiple of 6 and a multiple of 8. The common multiples of 6 and 8 follow an infinite pattern, 24, 48, 72, 96, 120, ... If the task is to find the least common multiple (LCM) of 6 and 8, the multiples of 6 and 8 are compared to find the smallest common multiple (other than zero), which is 24.

 Formative Assessment

To find out if a student understands the finding common multiples concept, ask the student to name at least five multiples of the following numbers;

5   7   12

Then ask the student to find at least two common multiple of the following pairs of numbers;

5, 15   4, 10   24, 16

Then ask the student to find the LCM of the following numbers;

5, 6, 15   50, 4, 20   24, 6, 15

Successful Strategies

One of the most beneficial ways to help students find the LCM is to have students show the multiples of each number in a skip counting pattern. When students examine these patterns it is easier to find the common multiples and the LCM. Students may show the multiples with numbers, words, or models. The hundred chart serves as a valuable tool in helping students to find common and least common multiples.

Math Words to Use
least, common, multiple, pattern

Questions at Different *Levels of Cognitive Demand*

EASY

Recall: *What is a multiple of 4?*

Comprehension: *Which examples could you give for the common multiples of 5 and 10?*

Application: *How would you show a pattern of common multiples?*

Analysis: *How would you compare the LCMs of two pairs of numbers?*

Evaluation: *What strategy would you recommend for finding the LCM?*

Synthesis: *When would it be necessary to find the LCM of four numbers?*

COMPLEX

LCM Hopscotch

A game designed to build the concept of finding common multiples

Materials:

- Two sets of 1-9 Numeral Cards
- Pawn for each player
- LCM Hopscotch Game Board
- LCM Hopscotch Spinner, paper clip

Directions:

1. Place pawns in the start position. Mix each set of numeral cards and place face-down in two piles.
2. The first player spins the spinner to find out if he will have a turn. For the first move, if the spinner lands on "Common multiples (not the least)" the player misses a turn. If the spinner lands on "Least common multiple" the player chooses one numeral card from each pile and flips them over. If the player names the correct LCM, he moves the pawn to the first space on the Hopscotch game board.
3. The next player takes a turn.
4. To make the second move on the Hopscotch board the player has to spin "Common multiples (not the least)." To move to this position, the player has to name two common multiples that are not the least.
5. Players continue taking turns, naming common multiples, and moving their pawns on the game board.
6. The winner is the first player to reach the top of the Hopscotch game board.

Content Differentiation:

Moving Back: Use 1-6 numeral cards.

Moving Ahead: Use three sets of numeral cards to find the LCM of three numbers.

1-9 Numeral Cards

· ·

1	2	3	4
5	<u>6</u>	7	8
<u>9</u>	1	2	3
4	5	<u>6</u>	7
8	<u>9</u>		

LCM Hopscotch Game Board

LCM

| A Common Multiple | A Different Common Multiple |

LCM

| A Common Multiple | A Different Common Multiple |

LCM

| A Common Multiple | A Different Common Multiple |

LCM

Start

LCM Hopscotch Spinner

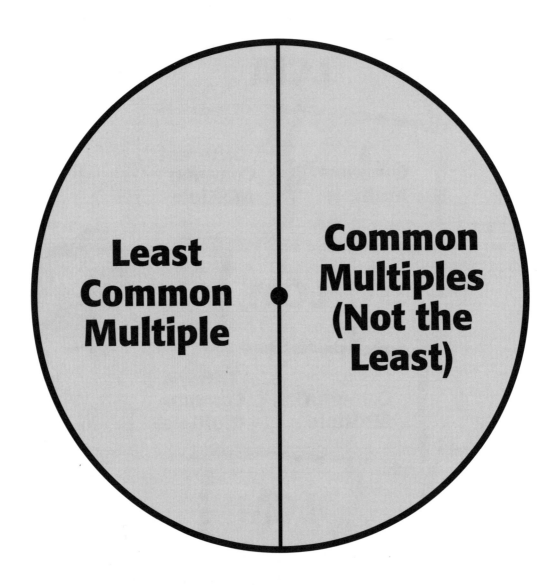

To use the spinner, place a paper clip in the center. Place pencil point through the paper clip at the center of the spinner. Holding the pencil securely with one hand, spin the paper clip with the other hand.

What is the Finding Common Factors Concept?

A factor of a number will divide that number evenly. For example, 9 is a factor of 18 because 18 can be divided by 9 without any remainders or fractional parts of a number. Eighteen has other factors, too. It is also divided evenly by 6 and 3, also by 1 and itself. The factors of 18 are 1, 2, 3, 6, 9, 18. If a number is *only* divisible by 1 and itself, it is a prime number. Often the task is to find common factors of two or more numbers. For example, 5 is a common factor of 30 and 20 because 5 is a factor of 30 and of 20. In fact, 1, 2, 5, 10 are all common factors of 30 and 20. If the task is to find the greatest common factor (GCF) of 30 and 20, we compare the factors of 30 and the factors of 20 to find the largest common factor, which is 10.

 Formative Assessment

To find out if a student understands the finding factors concept ask the student to name at least five factors of the following numbers;

12   50   48

Then ask the student to find at least two common factors of the following pairs of numbers;

15, 35   12, 18   36, 16

Then ask the student to find the GCF of the following numbers;

9, 12, 24   18, 48, 30   33, 7, 20

Successful Strategies

As with finding the LCM, a beneficial way to help students find the GCF is to have students show the factors of each number in a skip counting pattern. When students examine these patterns it is easier to find the common factors and the GCF. Students may show the factors with numbers, words, or models. The hundred chart serves as a valuable tool in helping students to find common and greatest common factors.

 ## Questions at Different *Levels of Cognitive Demand*

EASY

Recall: *What is a factor of 10?*

Comprehension: *Which examples could you give for the common factors of 10 and 8?*

Application: *How would you show the order of common factors?*

Analysis: *How would you compare the GCFs for two pairs of numbers?*

Evaluation: *What strategy do you recommend for finding the GCF?*

Synthesis: *What if we needed to find the GCF of four numbers?*

COMPLEX

GCF Hopscotch

*A game designed to build the concept
of finding common factors*

Materials:

PLAYERS:
2 OR MORE

- Two sets of GCF Numeral Cards
- Pawn for each player
- GCF Hopscotch Game Board
- GCF Hopscotch Spinner, paper clip

Directions:

1. Place pawns in the start position. Mix each set of GCF numeral cards and place cards face-down in two piles.
2. The first player spins the spinner to find out if she will have a turn. For the first move, if the spinner lands on "Common factors (not the greatest)" the player misses the turn. If the spinner lands on "Greatest common factor" the player chooses one numeral card from each pile and flips both cards over. If the player names the correct GCF, she moves the pawn to the first space on the Hopscotch game board.
3. The next player takes a turn.
4. To make the second move on the Hopscotch board the player has to spin "Common factors (not the greatest)." To move to this position, the player must name two common factors that are not the greatest. If it is not possible to name two common factors that are not the greatest the player misses the turn.
5. Players continue taking turns, naming common factors, and moving their pawns on the game board. The winner is the first player to reach the top of the Hopscotch game board.

Content Differentiation:

Moving Back: Use only lower value GCF numeral cards.

Moving Ahead: Use three sets of numeral cards to find the GCF of three numbers.

GCF Numeral Cards

· ·

4	<u>6</u>	8	<u>9</u>
10	12	14	15
16	18	20	21
24	25	28	30
32	35	36	40

GCF Hopscotch Game Board

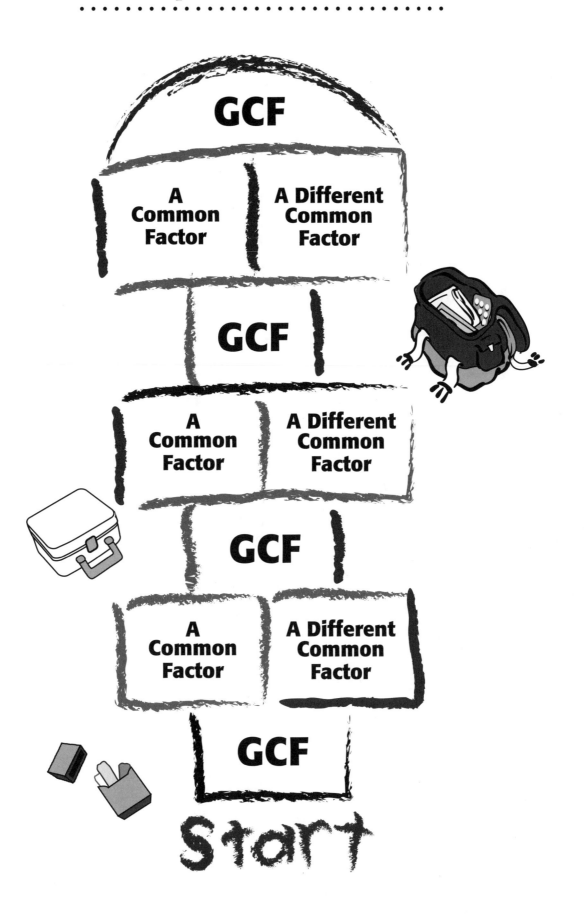

GCF

| A Common Factor | A Different Common Factor |

GCF

| A Common Factor | A Different Common Factor |

GCF

| A Common Factor | A Different Common Factor |

GCF

Start

GCF Hopscotch Spinner

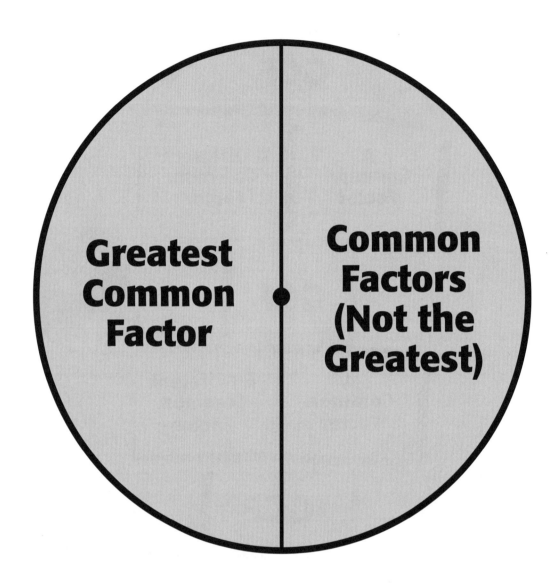

To use the spinner, place a paper clip in the center. Place pencil point through the paper clip at the center of the spinner. Holding the pencil securely with one hand, spin the paper clip with the other hand.

Adding and Subtracting Fractions

 What is the Adding and Subtracting Fractions Concept?

The addition and subtraction of fractions includes either fractions with like denominators or fractions that need to be renamed so that they have like denominators. Like denominators allow the computation focus to be on the numerators because we are working with the same size fractional parts, for example, $\frac{5}{8} + \frac{2}{8} = \frac{7}{8}$. Unlike denominators often require us to rename the fractions using the least common multiple or the greatest common factor of the denominators, for example, $\frac{3}{9} + \frac{3}{12}$. The GCF of 9 and 12 is 3. We can multiply the denominators and divide by the GCF (9 x 12 = 108, 108 ÷ 3 = 36). Or we can divide one of the denominators by the GCF and multiply the answer by the other denominator (9 ÷ 3 = 3, 3 x 12 = 36) to determine the common denominator. The fractions are renamed ($\frac{3}{9} = \frac{12}{36}, \frac{3}{12} = \frac{9}{36}$) using the LCM and the numerators are added, $\frac{12}{36} + \frac{9}{36} = \frac{21}{36}$. The fraction is simplified if possible, $\frac{21}{36} = \frac{7}{12}$. Students must do more than just follow the procedures. It is critical that they develop conceptual understanding of adding and subtracting fractions.

 Formative Assessment

To find out if a student knows how to add and subtract fractions ask the student to solve the following equations;

$\frac{1}{4} + \frac{2}{4} =$ $\frac{4}{5} - \frac{2}{5} =$

$\frac{1}{6} + \frac{2}{3} =$ $\frac{1}{2} - \frac{1}{4} =$

$\frac{6}{4} + \frac{1}{5} =$ $\frac{5}{3} - \frac{2}{4} =$

Successful Strategies

To help students understand why like denominators are important, students need meaningful experiences with comparing and ordering units. They should use fraction manipulatives such as fraction bars and fraction circles to enable them to learn the significance of using like denominators when computing fractions. Encourage students to work with equivalent fractions, which helps them build foundational understandings necessary for renaming fractions like denominators and simplifying fractions. Guide students through explorations of improper fractions, which is when the numerator is equal to or larger than the denominator.

> ## Math Words to Use
>
> fractions, rename,
> equivalent, numerator,
> denominator, improper,
> addition, subtraction,
> equation

 Questions at Different *Levels of Cognitive Demand*

EASY **Recall:** *What is $\frac{1}{3} + \frac{1}{3}$?*

Comprehension: *How would you explain a way to add halves and fourths?*

Application: *How would you show $\frac{3}{6} - \frac{1}{2}$ with fraction strips?*

Analysis: *What relationships are represented in the fractions of this equation; $\frac{1}{8} + \frac{1}{2} + \frac{3}{4}$?*

Evaluation: *How would you teach someone to add and subtract fractions?*

Synthesis: *What if you needed to subtract fractions*
COMPLEX *that had 3-digit denominators?*

Clothesline Fractions

*A game designed to build the concept
of adding and subtracting fractions*

PLAYERS: 2 OR MORE

Materials:

- **Clothesline (or thick string)**
- **Clothespins and Index cards**
- **4 dice (labeled 1-6 with numerals)**
- **Pencils and markers, a different color for each player**

Directions:

1. **Roll all four dice. Decide which numbers will be the numerators and which numbers will be the denominators.**
2. **Use the two fractions to make an addition equation. Write the equation on an index card. For example, $\frac{4}{3} + \frac{2}{6} = \frac{10}{6}$ or $\frac{5}{3}$. The player writes the sum with a marker.**
3. **The player uses a clothespin to hang the sum on the clothesline (which serves as a number line).**
4. **Players take turns rolling cubes, writing fraction equations, and hanging the cards on the number line.**
5. **Players score one point for every equivalent fraction hung on the clothesline.** *NOTE: Equivalent fractions are pinned under one another, not side-by-side on the number line, because they have the same value.*
6. **The first player to score four points is the winner. Play the game again using subtraction instead of addition.** *NOTE: Adjusting the spacing and placement of the index cards on the number line as the game progresses is an important process.*

Content Differentiation:

Moving Back: **Model each fraction equation with fraction strips.**

Moving Ahead: **Try the game using 1-10 spinners *(see page 98)* instead of dice.**

NOTE: A version of this game appears in Taylor-Cox, J. (2005)
***Family Math Night: Math Standards in Action.** Eye on Education.*

Rename Fractions as Decimals

· ·

 What is the Rename Fractions as Decimals Concept?

Decimal fractions are numbers that contain a decimal point. Some decimal fractions end with a specific number of places (terminating decimal, such as $\frac{1}{2}$ = .5). Some decimals have infinite repeating patterns (repeating decimal, such as $\frac{1}{3}$ = .33333...). When students rename fractions as decimals, they may think about money to put the fraction into a decimal context. For example, $\frac{1}{4}$ = one quarter of a dollar or .25. Students may visualize or use a number line. For example, $5\frac{1}{2}$ is exactly between 5 and 6 or 5.5. Students may think about an equivalent fraction that is tenths, hundreds, thousandths, etc. For example, $\frac{4}{20}$ is the same as $\frac{2}{10}$ or .20. Students may rename a fraction as a decimal by dividing the numerator by the denominator. For example, $\frac{6}{8}$ = .75.

 Formative Assessment

To find out if a student understands renaming fractions as decimals concept ask the student to rename the following fractions as decimals;

$\frac{1}{2}$ $\frac{3}{4}$ $\frac{3}{5}$

$\frac{10}{6}$ $\frac{20}{8}$ $2\frac{5}{4}$

Successful Strategies

It is beneficial for students to use multiple ways to rename fractions as decimals. When students only memorize procedures such as dividing the numerator by the denominator, the rule is not grounded in conceptual understanding; therefore it is not necessarily fully understood. Use multiple strategies (such as locating fractions on number lines and using fraction manipulatives to compare, order, and compute fractions) to help students understand what it means and why it is important to rename fraction as decimals.

> ### Math Words to Use
>
> **fractions, decimals, rename, numerator, denominator**

Questions at Different *Levels of Cognitive Demand*

EASY

Recall: *What decimal fraction is the same as $\frac{3}{4}$?*

Comprehension: *How did you rename the fraction as a decimal?*

Application: *How would you show the decimal with base ten blocks?*

Analysis: *Which fraction is smaller? How do you know?*

Evaluation: *Which fractions are more difficult to rename as decimals? Why?*

Synthesis: *How would you create a flowchart to organize renaming fractions as decimals?*

COMPLEX

Seven Up

*A game designed to build the concept
of renaming fractions as decimals*

Materials:

**PLAYERS:
2 OR MORE**

- Marker, a different color for each player
- Seven Up Game Board
- Centimeter cube
- Calculator for each player

Directions:

1. The first player holds the centimeter cube about 6 inches above the game board and drops it.
2. The rectangle that the cube covers most is the fraction that the player must rename as a decimal. The player must also identify the decimal as terminating or repeating. Players can use the calculator to rename the fractions as decimals.
3. If the player renames the fraction as a decimal accurately, the player uses her marker to draw X on the rectangle.
   NOTE: If the player accurately renames the fraction as a decimal without using the calculator, she may draw an additional X on any other rectangle.
4. Players use the calculator to verify one another's answers.
5. Players take turns dropping the cube and renaming fractions as decimals.
6. If a player drops the cube on a rectangle that already has an X, the player misses the turn.
7. The first player to have seven Xs in a vertical row (column) calls out "Seven Up!" to indicate that he is the winner.

Content Differentiation:

Moving Back: Rather than dropping the cubes, players choose fractions to rename.

Moving Ahead: Limit the number of times each player may use the calculator to rename fractions during the game.

Seven Up Game Board

$\frac{2}{4}$	$\frac{3}{6}$	$\frac{4}{8}$	$\frac{5}{10}$	$\frac{6}{12}$	$\frac{7}{14}$	$\frac{8}{16}$	$\frac{9}{18}$	$\frac{10}{20}$
$\frac{2}{6}$	$\frac{3}{9}$	$\frac{4}{12}$	$\frac{5}{15}$	$\frac{6}{18}$	$\frac{7}{21}$	$\frac{8}{24}$	$\frac{9}{27}$	$\frac{10}{30}$
$\frac{4}{6}$	$\frac{6}{9}$	$\frac{8}{12}$	$\frac{10}{15}$	$\frac{12}{18}$	$\frac{14}{21}$	$\frac{16}{24}$	$\frac{18}{27}$	$\frac{20}{30}$
$\frac{2}{8}$	$\frac{3}{12}$	$\frac{4}{16}$	$\frac{5}{20}$	$\frac{6}{24}$	$\frac{7}{28}$	$\frac{8}{32}$	$\frac{9}{36}$	$\frac{10}{40}$
$\frac{6}{8}$	$\frac{9}{12}$	$\frac{12}{16}$	$\frac{15}{20}$	$\frac{18}{24}$	$\frac{21}{28}$	$\frac{24}{32}$	$\frac{27}{36}$	$\frac{30}{40}$
$\frac{2}{10}$	$\frac{3}{15}$	$\frac{4}{20}$	$\frac{5}{25}$	$\frac{6}{30}$	$\frac{7}{35}$	$\frac{8}{40}$	$\frac{9}{45}$	$\frac{10}{50}$
$\frac{4}{10}$	$\frac{6}{15}$	$\frac{8}{20}$	$\frac{10}{26}$	$\frac{12}{30}$	$\frac{14}{35}$	$\frac{16}{40}$	$\frac{18}{45}$	$\frac{20}{50}$
$\frac{6}{10}$	$\frac{9}{15}$	$\frac{12}{20}$	$\frac{15}{25}$	$\frac{18}{30}$	$\frac{21}{35}$	$\frac{24}{40}$	$\frac{27}{45}$	$\frac{30}{50}$
$\frac{8}{10}$	$\frac{12}{15}$	$\frac{16}{20}$	$\frac{20}{25}$	$\frac{24}{30}$	$\frac{28}{35}$	$\frac{32}{40}$	$\frac{36}{45}$	$\frac{40}{50}$
$\frac{2}{12}$	$\frac{3}{18}$	$\frac{4}{24}$	$\frac{5}{30}$	$\frac{6}{36}$	$\frac{7}{42}$	$\frac{8}{48}$	$\frac{9}{54}$	$\frac{10}{60}$
$\frac{10}{12}$	$\frac{15}{18}$	$\frac{20}{24}$	$\frac{25}{30}$	$\frac{30}{36}$	$\frac{35}{42}$	$\frac{40}{48}$	$\frac{45}{54}$	$\frac{50}{60}$
$\frac{2}{16}$	$\frac{3}{24}$	$\frac{4}{32}$	$\frac{5}{40}$	$\frac{6}{48}$	$\frac{7}{56}$	$\frac{8}{64}$	$\frac{9}{72}$	$\frac{18}{80}$
$\frac{6}{16}$	$\frac{9}{24}$	$\frac{12}{32}$	$\frac{15}{40}$	$\frac{18}{48}$	$\frac{21}{56}$	$\frac{24}{64}$	$\frac{27}{72}$	$\frac{30}{80}$
$\frac{10}{16}$	$\frac{15}{24}$	$\frac{20}{32}$	$\frac{25}{40}$	$\frac{30}{48}$	$\frac{35}{56}$	$\frac{40}{64}$	$\frac{45}{72}$	$\frac{50}{80}$
$\frac{14}{16}$	$\frac{21}{24}$	$\frac{28}{32}$	$\frac{35}{40}$	$\frac{42}{48}$	$\frac{49}{56}$	$\frac{56}{64}$	$\frac{63}{72}$	$\frac{70}{80}$

Compare and Order Fractions and Mixed Numbers

 ## What is the Compare and Order Fractions and Mixed Numbers Concept?

Fractions name parts of wholes, units, or sets. A mixed number is a whole number and a fraction, such as $4\frac{1}{2}$. An improper fraction is a fraction that has a numerator that is equal to or larger than the denominator, such as $\frac{5}{4}$. To compare and order fractions and mixed numbers we often find equivalent fractions so that the comparisons are easier to make. Using a reference, such as $\frac{1}{2}$, often helps students to begin the comparison process.

 ## Formative Assessment

To find out if a student understands how to compare and order fractions and mixed numbers ask the student to put the three fractions in order from least to the greatest;

$$\frac{1}{2}, \ \frac{1}{3}, \ \frac{1}{4}$$

$$\frac{1}{16}, \ \frac{3}{8}, \ \frac{1}{4}$$

$$\frac{6}{10}, \ \frac{21}{50}, \ \frac{25}{100}$$

$$\frac{8}{3}, \ \frac{6}{4}, \ \frac{15}{8}$$

$$3\frac{1}{2}, \ 2\frac{8}{10}, \ 2\frac{1}{2}, \ 3\frac{3}{10}$$

Ask the student to explain how he knows the fractions are in order.

Successful Strategies

To help students strengthen their knowledge of equivalent fractions, use fraction strips to show how some fractions name the same number. It is meaningful for students to make their own sets of fraction strips. To do so, provide students with ruler-sized strips of paper that are all different colors. Each color represents a different denominator. Each full strip represents one whole. Encourage students to use comparing and folding to figure out where to cut the strips to show the fractional parts. After students are comfortable working with the strips, encourage them to use additional strips to show improper fractions and mixed numbers.

> ### Math Words to Use
>
> **fractions, improper fractions, mixed number, equivalent, order, compare, numerator, denominator**

Questions at Different *Levels of Cognitive Demand*

EASY

Recall: *What fraction is the same as $\frac{3}{6}$?*

Comprehension: *How would you describe improper fractions?*

Application: *How would you use fraction strips to show equivalent fractions?*

Analysis: *Which fraction is smaller? Larger? How do you know?*

Evaluation: *What is the best way to order mixed numbers and improper fractions?*

COMPLEX

Synthesis: *What if all the fractions were tripled?*

Lucky Ducky, Ducks in a Row

A game designed to build the concept of comparing and ordering fractions and mixed numbers

Materials:

PLAYERS: 2 OR MORE

- Ducks in a Row Fraction Cards (copied on yellow paper)
- Ducks in a Row Mixed Number Cards (copied on green paper)
- Ducks in a Row Improper Fractions Cards (copied on blue paper)
- 3 paper plates
- Dry erase board and marker for each player

Directions:

1. Cut out each set of cards. Place cards face-down on separate paper plates.
2. The first player flips over a card from each plate.
3. Players race to put the values in order from least to greatest. Players write their answers on dry erase boards.
4. The first player who arranges the values in order calls out, "Lucky Ducky!"
5. Other players verify the answer. If the player who called out "Lucky Ducky" has the correct order, he keeps all three cards. If the player is not correct, the cards go back to the plates.
6. Players take turns flipping cards and racing to put the values in order.
7. The winner is the first player to earn 24 cards.

Content Differentiation:

Moving Back: Draw two cards using only the fraction cards (yellow), mixed number card (green), improper fraction cards (blue), or make your own fraction cards.

Moving Ahead: Flip over two cards from each plate and order all six values or make your own fraction cards.

Ducks in a Row Fraction Cards
(copy on yellow paper)

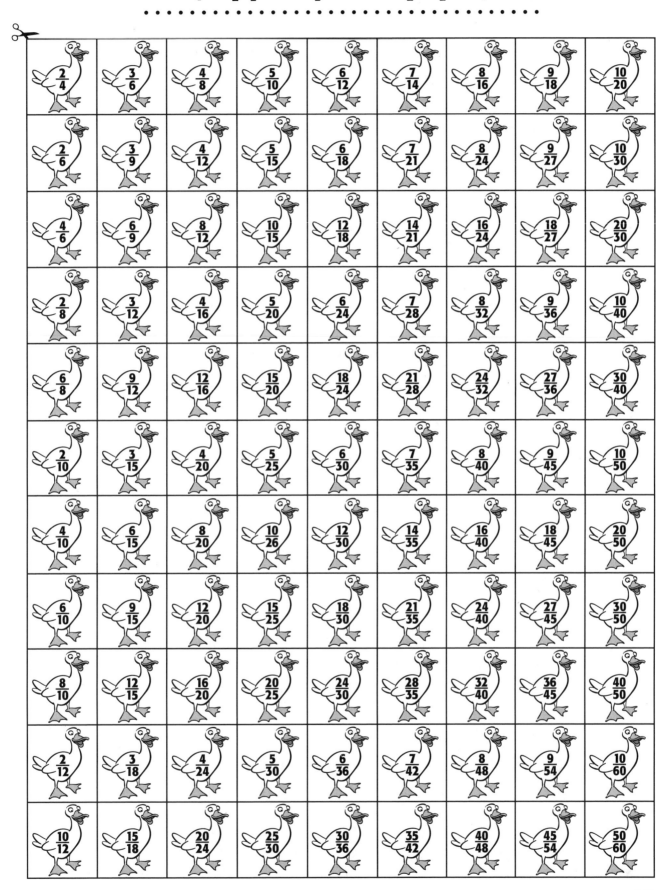

$\frac{2}{4}$	$\frac{3}{6}$	$\frac{4}{8}$	$\frac{5}{10}$	$\frac{6}{12}$	$\frac{7}{14}$	$\frac{8}{16}$	$\frac{9}{18}$	$\frac{10}{20}$
$\frac{2}{6}$	$\frac{3}{9}$	$\frac{4}{12}$	$\frac{5}{15}$	$\frac{6}{18}$	$\frac{7}{21}$	$\frac{8}{24}$	$\frac{9}{27}$	$\frac{10}{30}$
$\frac{4}{6}$	$\frac{6}{9}$	$\frac{8}{12}$	$\frac{10}{15}$	$\frac{12}{18}$	$\frac{14}{21}$	$\frac{16}{24}$	$\frac{18}{27}$	$\frac{20}{30}$
$\frac{2}{8}$	$\frac{3}{12}$	$\frac{4}{16}$	$\frac{5}{20}$	$\frac{6}{24}$	$\frac{7}{28}$	$\frac{8}{32}$	$\frac{9}{36}$	$\frac{10}{40}$
$\frac{6}{8}$	$\frac{9}{12}$	$\frac{12}{16}$	$\frac{15}{20}$	$\frac{18}{24}$	$\frac{21}{28}$	$\frac{24}{32}$	$\frac{27}{36}$	$\frac{30}{40}$
$\frac{2}{10}$	$\frac{3}{15}$	$\frac{4}{20}$	$\frac{5}{25}$	$\frac{6}{30}$	$\frac{7}{35}$	$\frac{8}{40}$	$\frac{9}{45}$	$\frac{10}{50}$
$\frac{4}{10}$	$\frac{6}{15}$	$\frac{8}{20}$	$\frac{10}{26}$	$\frac{12}{30}$	$\frac{14}{35}$	$\frac{16}{40}$	$\frac{18}{45}$	$\frac{20}{50}$
$\frac{6}{10}$	$\frac{9}{15}$	$\frac{12}{20}$	$\frac{15}{25}$	$\frac{18}{30}$	$\frac{21}{35}$	$\frac{24}{40}$	$\frac{27}{45}$	$\frac{30}{50}$
$\frac{8}{10}$	$\frac{12}{15}$	$\frac{16}{20}$	$\frac{20}{25}$	$\frac{24}{30}$	$\frac{28}{35}$	$\frac{32}{40}$	$\frac{36}{45}$	$\frac{40}{50}$
$\frac{2}{12}$	$\frac{3}{18}$	$\frac{4}{24}$	$\frac{5}{30}$	$\frac{6}{36}$	$\frac{7}{42}$	$\frac{8}{48}$	$\frac{9}{54}$	$\frac{10}{60}$
$\frac{10}{12}$	$\frac{15}{18}$	$\frac{20}{24}$	$\frac{25}{30}$	$\frac{30}{36}$	$\frac{35}{42}$	$\frac{40}{48}$	$\frac{45}{54}$	$\frac{50}{60}$

Ducks in a Row Mixed Number Cards
(copy on green paper)

$1\frac{2}{4}$	$2\frac{3}{6}$	$3\frac{4}{8}$	$1\frac{5}{10}$	$2\frac{6}{12}$	$3\frac{7}{14}$	$1\frac{8}{16}$	$2\frac{9}{18}$	$3\frac{10}{20}$
$1\frac{2}{6}$	$2\frac{3}{9}$	$3\frac{4}{12}$	$1\frac{5}{15}$	$2\frac{6}{18}$	$3\frac{7}{21}$	$1\frac{8}{24}$	$2\frac{9}{27}$	$3\frac{10}{30}$
$1\frac{4}{6}$	$2\frac{6}{9}$	$3\frac{8}{12}$	$1\frac{10}{15}$	$2\frac{12}{18}$	$3\frac{14}{21}$	$1\frac{16}{24}$	$2\frac{18}{27}$	$3\frac{20}{30}$
$1\frac{2}{8}$	$2\frac{3}{12}$	$3\frac{4}{16}$	$1\frac{5}{20}$	$2\frac{6}{24}$	$3\frac{7}{28}$	$1\frac{8}{32}$	$2\frac{9}{36}$	$3\frac{10}{40}$
$1\frac{6}{8}$	$2\frac{9}{12}$	$3\frac{12}{16}$	$1\frac{15}{20}$	$2\frac{18}{24}$	$3\frac{21}{28}$	$1\frac{24}{32}$	$2\frac{27}{36}$	$3\frac{30}{40}$
$1\frac{2}{10}$	$2\frac{3}{15}$	$3\frac{4}{20}$	$1\frac{5}{25}$	$2\frac{6}{30}$	$3\frac{7}{35}$	$1\frac{8}{40}$	$2\frac{9}{45}$	$3\frac{10}{50}$
$1\frac{4}{10}$	$2\frac{6}{15}$	$3\frac{8}{20}$	$1\frac{10}{26}$	$2\frac{12}{30}$	$3\frac{14}{35}$	$1\frac{16}{40}$	$2\frac{18}{45}$	$3\frac{20}{50}$
$1\frac{6}{10}$	$2\frac{9}{15}$	$3\frac{12}{20}$	$1\frac{15}{25}$	$2\frac{18}{30}$	$3\frac{21}{35}$	$1\frac{24}{40}$	$2\frac{27}{45}$	$3\frac{30}{50}$
$1\frac{8}{10}$	$2\frac{12}{15}$	$3\frac{16}{20}$	$1\frac{20}{25}$	$2\frac{24}{30}$	$3\frac{28}{35}$	$1\frac{32}{40}$	$2\frac{36}{45}$	$3\frac{40}{50}$
$1\frac{2}{12}$	$2\frac{3}{18}$	$3\frac{4}{24}$	$1\frac{5}{30}$	$2\frac{6}{36}$	$3\frac{7}{42}$	$1\frac{8}{48}$	$2\frac{9}{54}$	$3\frac{10}{60}$
$1\frac{10}{12}$	$2\frac{15}{18}$	$3\frac{20}{24}$	$1\frac{25}{30}$	$2\frac{30}{36}$	$3\frac{35}{42}$	$1\frac{40}{48}$	$2\frac{45}{54}$	$3\frac{50}{60}$

Ducks in a Row Improper Fraction Cards
(copy on blue paper)

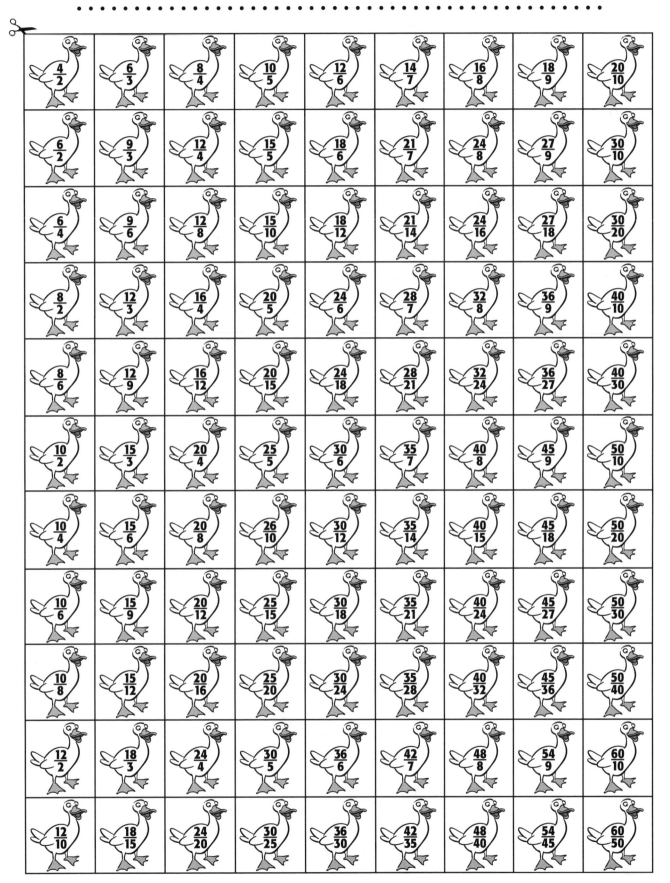

$\frac{4}{2}$	$\frac{6}{3}$	$\frac{8}{4}$	$\frac{10}{5}$	$\frac{12}{6}$	$\frac{14}{7}$	$\frac{16}{8}$	$\frac{18}{9}$	$\frac{20}{10}$
$\frac{6}{2}$	$\frac{9}{3}$	$\frac{12}{4}$	$\frac{15}{5}$	$\frac{18}{6}$	$\frac{21}{7}$	$\frac{24}{8}$	$\frac{27}{9}$	$\frac{30}{10}$
$\frac{6}{4}$	$\frac{9}{6}$	$\frac{12}{8}$	$\frac{15}{10}$	$\frac{18}{12}$	$\frac{21}{14}$	$\frac{24}{16}$	$\frac{27}{18}$	$\frac{30}{20}$
$\frac{8}{2}$	$\frac{12}{3}$	$\frac{16}{4}$	$\frac{20}{5}$	$\frac{24}{6}$	$\frac{28}{7}$	$\frac{32}{8}$	$\frac{36}{9}$	$\frac{40}{10}$
$\frac{8}{6}$	$\frac{12}{9}$	$\frac{16}{12}$	$\frac{20}{15}$	$\frac{24}{18}$	$\frac{28}{21}$	$\frac{32}{24}$	$\frac{36}{27}$	$\frac{40}{30}$
$\frac{10}{2}$	$\frac{15}{3}$	$\frac{20}{4}$	$\frac{25}{5}$	$\frac{30}{6}$	$\frac{35}{7}$	$\frac{40}{8}$	$\frac{45}{9}$	$\frac{50}{10}$
$\frac{10}{4}$	$\frac{15}{6}$	$\frac{20}{8}$	$\frac{26}{10}$	$\frac{30}{12}$	$\frac{35}{14}$	$\frac{40}{15}$	$\frac{45}{18}$	$\frac{50}{20}$
$\frac{10}{6}$	$\frac{15}{9}$	$\frac{20}{12}$	$\frac{25}{15}$	$\frac{30}{18}$	$\frac{35}{21}$	$\frac{40}{24}$	$\frac{45}{27}$	$\frac{50}{30}$
$\frac{10}{8}$	$\frac{15}{12}$	$\frac{20}{16}$	$\frac{25}{20}$	$\frac{30}{24}$	$\frac{35}{28}$	$\frac{40}{32}$	$\frac{45}{36}$	$\frac{50}{40}$
$\frac{12}{2}$	$\frac{18}{3}$	$\frac{24}{4}$	$\frac{30}{5}$	$\frac{36}{6}$	$\frac{42}{7}$	$\frac{48}{8}$	$\frac{54}{9}$	$\frac{60}{10}$
$\frac{12}{10}$	$\frac{18}{15}$	$\frac{24}{20}$	$\frac{30}{25}$	$\frac{36}{30}$	$\frac{42}{35}$	$\frac{48}{40}$	$\frac{54}{45}$	$\frac{60}{50}$

Ducks in a Row Make Your Own
Fraction Cards

· ·

Notes

Notes

Notes

Notes

References

Bermejo, V. (1996). Cardinality Development and Counting. *Developmental Psychology*, vol. 32, no. 2, pp 263-268.

Bloom, B., Englehart, M. Furst, E., Hill, W., & Krathwohl, D. (1956). Taxonomy of Educational Objectives; The Classification of Educational Goals. *Handbook I: Cognitive Domain*. New York, Toronto: Longmans Green.

Clements, D. (1999). Subitizing: What is it? Why teach it? *Teaching Children Mathematics*, 5 (March): 400-405.

Freeman, F. N. (1912). Grouped Objects as a Concrete Basis for the Number Idea. *Elementary School Teacher* 8, 306-314.

Kaufman, E. L., Lord, M.W., Reese, T. W. & Volkman, J. (1949). The Discrimination of Visual Number. *American Journal of Psychology*, 62, 498-525.

McIntosh, A. J., Reyes, B. J., and Reys, R. E. (1993). A Proposed Framework for Examining Number Sense. *For the Learning of Mathematics*, 12 (3), 2-8.

National Association for the Education of Young Children and National Council of Teachers of Mathematics. 2002. *Early Childhood Mathematics: Promoting Good Beginnings, A Joint Position Statement.* Reston, VA: NCTM.

National Council of Teachers of Mathematics (NCTM). *Curriculum Focal Points for Prekindergarten Through Grade 8 Mathematics: A Quest for Coherence.* Reston, VA: NCTM, 2006.

National Council of Teachers of Mathematics (NCTM). *Principles and Standards for School Mathematics.* Reston, VA: NCTM, 2000.

National Mathematics Advisory Panel (2008). *Foundations for Success: The Final Report of the National Mathematics Advisory Panel*, U.S. Department of Education: Washington, DC.

OED2, *Oxford English Dictionary, Second Edition Online*. New York, New York: Oxford University Press.

Piaget, J. (1964). Development and Learning. In R. Ripple & V. Rockcastle (Eds.). *Piaget Rediscovered*. Ithaca New York: Cornell University Press.

Piaget, J. (1970). Piaget's Theory. In P.H. Mussen (Ed.). *Carmichael's Manual of Child Psychology*, vol. 1, 3rd edition. London: John Wiley and Sons, Ins.

Taylor-Cox, J. (2001). How Many Marbles in the Jar? Estimation in the Early Grades. *Teaching Children Mathematics*, 8 (4), 208-2 14.

Taylor-Cox, J. (2005). *Family Math Night: Math Standards in Action*. Larchmont, NY: Eye on Education.

Taylor-Cox, J. & Kelly, B. (2008). The Doctors Disagree: Two Points of View on the Topic of "Drill and Kill" in Mathematics Education. *The Banneker Banner; The Official Journal of the Maryland Council of Teachers of Mathematics*, 25 (1), 6-7.